SCREENS

Electronic Mediations

Katherine Hayles, Mark Poster, and Samuel Weber, Series Editors

(continued on page 122)

SCREENS Viewing Media Installation Art

Kate Mondloch

Electronic Mediations, Volume 30

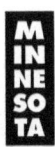

University of Minnesota Press
Minneapolis • London

Parts of chapters 1 and 4 were previously published in "Be Here (and There) Now: The Spatial Dynamics of Screen-Reliant Installation Art," *Art Journal* 66, no. 3 (2007): 20–33.

The art on the front cover of the paperback edition is by Günther Selichar: *Screen, cold #19*, (1997/2003), Ilfochrome/Alucobond, 125 x 162 cm; courtesy of Collection of the City of Vienna and VBK, Vienna. *Screen, cold #7*, (1997/2003), Ilfochrome/Alucobond, 125 x 163 cm; courtesy of private collection, Vienna, and VBK, Vienna. *Screen, cold #8*, (1997/2003), Ilfochrome/Alucobond, 125 x 167 cm; courtesy of Collection Maison Européenne de la Photographie, Paris, and VBK, Vienna. Copyright 2009 Artists Rights Society (ARS), New York / VBK, Vienna. http://selichar.net.

Published by the University of Minnesota Press
111 Third Avenue South, Suite 290
Minneapolis, MN 55401-2520
http://www.upress.umn.edu

Library of Congress Cataloging-in-Publication Data

Mondloch, Kate.
Screens : viewing media installation art / Kate Mondloch.
p.   cm. — (Electronic mediations ; v. 30)
Includes bibliographical references and index.
ISBN 978-0-8166-6521-1 (hc : alk. paper) —
ISBN 978-0-8166-6522-8 (pb : alk. paper)
1. Video installations (Art).   2. Image (Philosophy).
3. Art exhibition audiences.   I. Title.
N6494.V53M66   2010
776—dc22
2009007783

Printed in the United States of America on acid-free paper

The University of Minnesota is an equal-opportunity educator and employer.

16 15 14 13 12 11 10   10 9 8 7 6 5 4 3 2 1

FOR A. and the bug in his screen

The work of art might be said to build a garden

around the house of Being, and—in so doing—

make it what it could not otherwise be:

a site to which other men and women may journey to look.

—KAJA SILVERMAN, *World Spectators*

CONTENTS

Acknowledgments

It is a daunting charge to attempt to thank adequately all of the people who, in ways both small and monumental, helped me to write this book. Miwon Kwon deserves special recognition for nurturing this project in its nascent stages, and Jennifer Marshall and Chon Noriega share the distinction of being my most stalwart advocates and critics throughout the writing process. I am especially grateful for a series of timely and productive exchanges with Mike Aronson, Eric de Bruyn, Cindy Colburn, Mary Francis, Anne Friedberg, Colin Gardner, Ray Guins, Amelie Hastie, Kate Hayles, Erkki Huhtamo, David Joselit, Kathleen Karlyn, Liz Kotz, Samantha Lackey, Kent Minturn, Priscilla Ovalle, Judith Rodenbeck, Andy Schulz, Carol Stabile, Tamara Trodd, Sherry Turkle, Andrew Uroskie, Tony Vidler, and Michele White. Audiences at UCLA, UC Berkeley, the New American Art Union, Pepperdine University, and Stanford University offered insightful advice when I presented aspects of this project, as did the editorial boards at *Art Journal* and *Vectors*. My colleagues in the "Object of Media Studies" residential research group at the University of California Humanities Research Institute were inspiring interlocutors at a pivotal point in my research, and I am grateful for our continued collaboration. My many friends and colleagues at the University of Oregon have made my job a pleasure since I joined the faculty in 2005; at the risk of sounding clichéd, I couldn't have asked for a more welcoming or collegial group. I owe special thanks to Dean Frances Bronet and art history department chairs Sherwin Simmons and Charles Lachman for helping me to secure the institutional resources that allowed me to complete the final phases of the project. I am also grateful for the intellectual stimulation and ready humor of my students.

Among them, Dana Spencer has been an indefatigable research assistant in the arduous task of securing images and permissions, and Kim Hong graciously assisted with the final stages of the manuscript preparation.

The research and writing for this project have been supported by generous grants and fellowships from the University of California Humanities Research Institute, the Oregon Humanities Center (thanks especially to Barbara Altmann, Julia Heydon, and Steven Shankman), and the University of Oregon School of Architecture and Allied Arts. I would also like to acknowledge Liska Chan, Don Metz, Steina and Woody Vasulka, Anthology Film Archives, Artists Rights Society, the Generali Foundation, and the ZKM | Center for Art and Media for assisting me with images and for allowing me access to important archives. I am indebted to Günther Selichar for granting permission to reproduce his artwork on the book's cover. Additional thanks are due my editor, Doug Armato, and series editors Katherine Hayles, Samuel Weber, and Mark Poster; their collective enthusiasm and encouragement have been invaluable. Editorial assistant Danielle Kasprzak, copy editors Nancy Sauro and Michele Hodgson, and the entire staff at the University of Minnesota Press worked diligently and attentively at every stage of the book's production, for which I am grateful. Finally, I'd like to thank the artists whose work inspired this book: it has been a delight to spend so much time in the company of their thought-provoking creations. The book's epigraph is for them.

My deepest gratitude is reserved for my family. Relatives on both sides of the Atlantic patiently listened to my ruminations about art and everything else with a combination of sincere appreciation and affable jesting when I needed them most. My parents have walked beside me in innumerable endeavors, lending their support and boundless optimism in myriad ways. Their resilience in the face of intolerable loss and grief continues to inspire me. I owe a special thanks to Oliver for the joy he brings me every day (spontaneous poetry included). Last, I would like to thank Andrea. He, above everyone else, has made every step of the journey a celebration.

Introduction Screen Subjects

As they have mediated our engagement with the world, with others, and with ourselves, cinematic and electronic technologies have transformed us so that we currently see, sense, and make sense of ourselves as quite other than we were before them.

—VIVIAN SOBCHACK, "The Scene of the Screen"

Media screens—film screens, video screens, computer screens, and the like—pervade contemporary life, characterizing both work and leisure moments. If in earlier times our sense of self was constructed through language, discourse, or a print-based culture, the screen-based interfaces that define countless forms of communication between subjects have made us, as the epigraph by Vivian Sobchack suggests, "quite other than we were before."[1] The film scholar's influential work exemplifies the mounting interest in theorizing the impact of media technologies on modes of vision and, indeed, on contemporary subjectivity. While there is a growing body of literature on screen-mediated visuality and its consequences in relationship to everyday media culture, relatively little has been written from the perspective of art and its history, even as screens and their technological apparatuses have become ever more prevalent in artistic production since the 1960s.[2] *Screens: Viewing Media Installation Art* contributes to existing theories of art, film, and media spectatorship by analyzing the particular relevance of screen-based viewing within the institutional context of the visual arts, specifically as revealed in installations made with media screens.

As in everyday life, screens are increasingly ubiquitous in art institutions worldwide. From historical survey shows dedicated to the seminal projected image works created in the 1960s and 1970s, such as Chrissie Iles's *Into the Light* (Whitney Museum, 2001) or Matthias Michalka's *X-Screen*

(Museum Moderner Kunst, 2003), to wide-ranging reviews of more recent art, such as Okwui Enwezor's *Documenta XI* (2002), Peter Weibel and Jeffrey Shaw's *Future Cinema* (ZKM, 2003) or Maria de Corral and Rosa Martinez's *51st Venice Biennale* (2005), art exhibitions now habitually reconfigure so-called white cube gallery spaces into "black boxes" for viewing screen-based art.[3] In part, the institutional recognition of projected and moving-image installations, and artistic experimentation with the genre itself, reflects concurrent changes in dominant commercial screen-based technologies.[4] Media installation's early years were largely characterized by modest 16 mm films displayed across one or more surfaces and ungainly video monitors featuring blurry black-and-white imagery. Nearly fifty years later, sleek, high-definition digital projections and architectural-scale screens have colonized gallery spaces and exhibitions across the globe.

Screens themselves, however, are decidedly ambivalent objects—illusionist windows and physical, material entities at the same time. "A screen is a barrier," wrote philosopher Stanley Cavell in 1971. "It screens me from the world it holds—that is, screens its existence from me."[5] Cavell was writing of the cinema, but his words are incisive for contemporary art criticism, too, particularly in an era in which artworks incorporating screens of all kinds permeate galleries and museums. Embellished with luminous images dancing across any number of surfaces, screens beckon, provoke, separate, and seduce. Yet the nature of viewing artworks made with these technological interfaces, along with their important subjective effects, remains largely unexplored.

One might begin such a critical project, as this book does, by closely examining the modes of spectatorship proposed in artworks that have incorporated viewer–screen interfaces over the past forty years. *Screens* focuses on European and North American installations made with cinematic and electronic screens from the late 1960s to the present, concentrating on case studies of particularly instructive pieces by Eija-Liisa Ahtila, Doug Aitken, Peter Campus, VALIE EXPORT, Dan Graham, Bruce Nauman, Michael Snow, and others. The book's ambition is twofold: it looks at the use of film, video, and computer screens as actual art objects, but it also builds on this to take into account the ways in which contemporary viewing subjects are themselves defined by interactions with screens. As such, *Screens* is not an encyclopedic history of media installation. Rather, through close study of exemplary artworks, the book introduces a theoretical model for thinking about this pervasive mode of contemporary artistic production: what I call screen-reliant installation art.[6] By investigating how artworks made with screen-based imaging and projection technologies stage vision and create distinctive experiences of sight, communication, and knowledge, the book also examines what artistic experimentation with screens might reveal about the changing relationship between contemporary viewers and their media technologies.

Screen-mediated art viewing existed well before the invention of still or moving photographic media. Indeed, artistic screens have arguably had an implied theoretical or virtual component in addition to their mundane physical concreteness ever since Leon Battista Alberti's fifteenth-century formulation of the canvas/screen as a window that opens onto a space "beyond the frame." Camera obscura images, shadow shows, magic lantern projections, panoramas, dioramas, and a variety of peep-show-based attractions also positioned their observers in front of "screens" of various kinds.[7] In this sense, contemporary forms of screen-based presentation are but the latest chapter of a long-standing practice in art production and reception. But an important shift occurs in art spectatorship when *mass media* screens are incorporated into environmental artworks (or "installations") in the mid-1960s, inaugurating a far-reaching exploration of art and media technologies of visualization. While the genre of installation art will be familiar to an art historical audience, it warrants a brief description here. Installation often overlaps with other post-1960 genres, such as fluxus, land art, minimalism, video art, performance, conceptual art, and process, all of which share an interest in issues such as site specificity, participation, institutional critique, temporality, and ephemerality. Installation artworks are participatory sculptural environments in which the viewer's spatial and temporal experience with the exhibition space and the various objects within it forms part of the work itself.[8] These pieces are meant to be experienced as activated spaces rather than as discrete objects: they are designed to "unfold" during the spectator's experience in time rather than to be known visually all at once. Installations made with media screens are especially evocative in that as environmental, experiential sculptures, they stage temporal and spatialized encounters between viewing subjects and technological objects, between bodies and screens. A potentially new mode of screen-reliant spectatorship emerges in the process.[9]

As a spectatorship study, the book's conceit is that *how* one sees is just as important as *what* one sees. Theories of spectatorship argue that visual (artistic) production actively produces particular ways of seeing.[10] To study spectatorship, then, is to consider how individuals look at representations as well as how they understand the setting and their experiences. In the case of film and media studies, theorizations of spectatorship recognize that neither media technologies nor the act of viewing them are unbiased. Instead, such critical methods demonstrate how viewers are rendered and regulated by institutions, technological apparatuses, and their representations. Film scholar Judith Mayne offers a concise definition of this line of inquiry in her *Cinema and Spectatorship:* "Spectatorship denotes a preoccupation with the various ways in which responses to films are constructed by the institutions of the cinema and with the contexts—psychic as well as cultural, individual as well as social—that give those responses particular meanings."[11] Critically assessing these conditions is especially important because how viewers are constructed generates effects even after they disengage from a specific work or representation. Hence, Sobchack's challenging contention about cinematic and electronic viewing technologies in the epigraph—"[they] have transformed us so that we currently see, sense, and make sense of ourselves as quite other than we were before them."

The term "spectatorship" further signals an investment in the theoretical points of overlap between Marxist, semiotic, feminist, and psychoanalytic critiques of visual culture and in apparatus and feminist film theory in particular.[12] These theories define how cinema works as an institutional system and center on analyses of the ideological, psychoanalytic, and phenomenological subject positions thus produced. It is worth emphasizing that spectatorial positions are not intended to describe the experience of any single individual but to suggest that all viewers are addressed and constructed by media forms. Film theorists typically make a distinction between the "subject" (the position assigned to the observer by the film and various cinematic codes) and the "viewer" (the actual person who watches the film and his or her complex viewing responses). Following Mayne, however, I employ the term "spectator" as a way to signal the unresolved difficulty of separating the subject from actual individuals; I use the terms "spectator" and "viewer" interchangeably in the text to further reinforce this point.[13] The book's primary concern is to investigate what kind of spectatorship these works propose in their specific cultural, individual, and artistic contexts rather than to argue that a single model unfailingly "works."[14]

While apparatus and feminist psychoanalytic film theory offer the most comprehensive critical approaches to the study of screen-reliant installation, inasmuch as they bring out the specific material and psychic aspects of engagement as well as the contribution of the screen object itself, these institutional models are not without their limitations.[15] Sobchack pinpoints

the shortcomings of recent film theory's reliance on a trilogy of unsatis-
factory metaphors—the formalist model of the picture frame, the realist
model of the window, and the poststructuralist model of the mirror—for
understanding the cinematic experience. The problem, as Sobchack sees
it, lies in how "all three metaphors relate directly to the screen rectangle
and to the film as a static *viewed object*, and only indirectly to the dynamic
activity of viewing that is engaged in by both the film and the spectator,
each as *viewing subjects*."[16] New phenomenological work in film and media
theory by Mark B. N. Hansen, Laura Marks, and Kaja Silverman, among
others, has addressed this lacuna.[17] By focusing on the affective and phenomenological consequences of viewing screen-based representations, these
methodologies, in conjunction with institutional models, offer the most
compelling way to analyze art and media institutions alongside their possible excesses and resistances.

Screens is thus situated at the intersection between art history and
film and media studies. It provides a much-needed reevaluation of influential yet understudied artworks created over the past forty years, works that
traditionally have been situated at the periphery of both fields and seldom
appear in book-length studies. Historical and theoretical treatments of
installation art by Michael Archer, Claire Bishop, Rosalind Krauss, and
Julie Reiss, among others, offer useful ways to think about the genre in
general, as well as the conceptual and phenomenological spaces peculiar to
its spectatorship.[18] Scholars in art history and film and media studies recently
have begun to assess the concerns particular to media installation art—
including incisive critiques focused on film and video environments since
the 1990s by such figures as Daniel Birnbaum, Raymond Bellour, and
Dominique Païni, as well as critical histories focused on the previously
neglected genres of expanded cinema and artists' films in the 1960s and
1970s by historians and critics, including Eric de Bruyn, Branden Joseph,
and Liz Kotz.[19] However, as writers in both disciplines have tended to
limit their investigations to works that share a single material basis or
"medium," such as works created with film *or* video *or* digital media, they
have neglected the provocative links and differences between them that
are among the foundational concerns of the present study.[20]

Faced with the current dominance of screen-based artistic production,
many art critics have pointed to a "filmic turn," some going so far as to por-
tray this as a sort of crisis for art criticism and history. Such was the symp-
tomatic claim of a roundtable discussion published in *October* magazine in

Spring 2003, whose participants warned: "We are now witnessing an intense relativization of the field of the art institution, the art critics, and the art historian by film history, cinema history, film theory."[21] Yet even if film history and theory are depicted as a threat, their methods have proven inadequate to understanding gallery-based media installations. Screen-reliant installations are not so much a wholesale defection away from the concerns and institutions specific to visual art as they are a provocative fusion of filmic/cinematic (or, more broadly, moving-image media) *and* artistic/sculptural concerns.

The majority of recent critical accounts focus on art's relationship to cinema, typically championing the presumed criticality of the viewer's encounter with advanced sculptural projects while disdaining the viewer's allegedly uncritical and passive experience with mainstream cinema. *Screens* eschews this dualistic thinking and examines the screen interface shared by artworks created with a range of media technologies. This approach allows the book to distinguish a generalized and momentous shift in post-1960 spectatorship brought about by technological objects that literally and metaphorically filter the observing subject's field of vision. This is not to say that all screens or techniques of screening are indistinguishable. Even in the "age of (digital) convergence," cinema, video, and the computer maintain significant differences in audiences, economics, and ideological origins.[22] Nevertheless, it is pivotal to recognize that the contemporary spectator's relationship to much visual production is indeed arbitrated by screens. To assess the viewer–screen interface as shared by environmental artworks across various genres and with a range of technologies (video, film, slide projection, and so on) is not to argue that there are no meaningful distinctions among screen-based apparatuses. Instead, *Screens* suggests that the particular technologies used in these pieces are less important than the kind of spectatorship proposed across a range of screen-based works and the implications of this for the spectatorial address of media installation art.

Anne Friedberg's pioneering cultural history of screen-based information surfaces, *The Virtual Window: From Alberti to Microsoft* (2006), serves as a primary reference point for the present study. *Screens* augments this research by emphasizing the unconventional uses of media screens and the curious mutations of the virtual-window paradigm in gallery-based installations. In this way, highlighting the processes and networks of screen-reliant art spectatorship provides a way to complicate dominant narratives about modes of media viewing and cultural norms.

The past several years have seen a steady rise of critical interest in both media art and so-called "screen studies."[23] The nascent field of screen studies, housed in disciplines ranging from new media studies to communications, contends with film, television, and computer screens in relationship to commercial mass media culture, but tends to overlook their highly particular uses within the institutional context of the visual arts. Operating outside this restrictive approach, Friedberg's *The Virtual Window* and Lev Manovich's *The Language of New Media* (2001) each devote chapters to analyzing how audiences view screen-based art, and Erkki Huhtamo has written a series of foundational essays analyzing the archaeology of the screen, including its artistic contexts.[24]

Apart from these important exceptions, however, the central organizing role of the screen as a technical device that informs how we experience much contemporary art for the most part has remained neglected by the field to which it matters most: art history. Given that screens have been the object of rigorous material and conceptual investigation in art since the 1960s, media installations offer a privileged entry point to the study of screen-reliant visuality. Simply put, the ways in which spectators engage screen-based technologies can be bracketed out, such that the terms of this engagement themselves are put on display in the art gallery and to critical effect. Whether or not an artist *consciously* investigates the conditions of media screen spectatorship, screen-reliant sculptural installations draw attention to the typically overlooked viewer–screen interface—the conceptual and material point at which the observing subject meets the technological object—and thereby open a space to consider critically the nature of contemporary screen-mediated viewing.

The interest of *Screens* is to emphasize the materiality of the experience of viewing screens in an art gallery setting and to situate it within a wider, transformational field of phenomenological, psychic, institutional, and ideological effects. Taking a cue from the artworks themselves, the book's thematic analysis of screen-reliant spectatorship draws out the typically obscured relationship between bodies, sites, and the objecthood of the screen-based apparatus. Thus, *Screens* invigorates screen studies. It offers the unique critical leverage of art, and the special interpretive models of art criticism and history, as an alternative way to understand media culture and contemporary visuality. This is not to suggest that the deployment of mass media screens in sculptural installations is in any way inherently oppositional or resistant. On the contrary, in what follows I have tried to acknowledge the range of ways in which art spectators both construct and are constructed by their interactions with media screens. To this end, I emphasize noteworthy conditions present in certain, but by no means all, moving-image installations to give a sense of the full range of possibilities.

The book is organized into five thematic chapters, each of which explores the operative mechanisms of screen spectatorship through two or more case studies of paradigmatic artworks. This thematic structure addresses the overall significance of the body–screen interface in media installation; the specific case studies allow a comparative analysis of individual screen-reliant artworks assessed in their material specificity. It begins by investigating the idea of the screen itself, then focuses on the qualitative, temporal, and spatial dimensions of media screen-based viewing in contemporary art.

Chapter 1, "Interface Matters," introduces the category of screen-reliant installation art as a way both to produce and to critique gallery-based media art since the late 1960s. Artists have critically reevaluated the screen and its functions by redeploying media technologies within the institutional context of the visual arts. The chapter begins by examining two experimental film works created by Paul Sharits— *T,O,U,C,H,I,N,G* (1968) and *Soundstrip/Filmstrip* (1971–72)—and considers the diverse models of spectatorship proposed in each as emblematic of the differences between experimental film and film installation. Next, I discuss Michael Snow's well-known film environment *Two Sides to Every Story* (1974). In this piece, two versions of a single film are projected onto opposite sides of a rectangular aluminum screen suspended prominently in the middle of the gallery space. The work's projected images operate cinematically, drawing the spectator into the film's illusionist space and theatrical mode of viewing. However, the installation's mode of presentation—two films of the same event projected onto opposing sides of a single screen that hovers mid-air in the center of the room—works to quite different effect, complicating and confounding theatrical cinematic spectatorship. Like *Soundstrip/ Filmstrip,* this work proposes a dynamic interaction between the place of the viewing subject, the film apparatus, and the representations on the screen. These gallery-based media works are ongoing screen-based material objects open to manifold readings, not simply at the level of the moving imagery but also in response to the real presence of the art objects in space. As such, they exemplify the strand of post-1960s media art examined in *Screens.*

"Body and Screen," chapter 2, scrutinizes the screen's decisive role in orchestrating the spectator's physical interaction with sculptural screen-based works. How do these media objects and their customary viewing regimes actively define the relationship between bodies and screens? This chapter complicates the notion of an inherently progressive, liberatory "spectator participation" that is celebrated in many accounts of installation art by detailing the ways in which media screens are also capable of generating oppressive viewing conditions that strictly delimit the viewer's interaction with the work. As in everyday life, screens and their illuminated moving images can offer a sort of siren song—calling spectators to largely involuntary behavior, entreating them to look and pay attention and to discipline themselves and their bodies in the process.

The chapter analyzes a series of influential closed-circuit video installations that intentionally explore the "architectures" of media spectatorship, including Frank Gillette and Ira Schneider's pioneering *Wipe Cycle* (1969), Bruce Nauman's video corridor works (1969–72), and Dan Graham's *Present Continuous Past(s)* (1974). Considering each of the projects in turn, this chapter analyzes how these early video installations fuse two seemingly incompatible processes. Artists underscore the coercive nature of screen-based viewing by varying the arrangement of cameras and monitors, combining live and prerecorded feedback, inverting viewers' images, divorcing cameras from their monitors, introducing time delays, and so on. Simultaneously, however, the technological apparatuses themselves arguably impose precise kinesthetic and psychic effects on their audiences.

"Installing Time," chapter 3, assesses how time is used as a material in more recent film and video installations and to what critical end. It extends the previous chapter's analysis of the charged relationship between bodies and screens by drawing attention to an aspect that remains undertheorized—the multiple and sometimes contradictory temporal impulses at work in the presentation of spatialized moving images to moving bodies. This section evaluates attempts to "install time" in space, and thereby put time itself on display, in influential pieces by Eija-Liisa Ahtila (*Consolation Service*, 1999), Doug Aitken (*electric earth*, 1999), Douglas Gordon (*24 Hour Psycho*, 1993), and Bruce Nauman [*Mapping the Studio I (Fat Chance John Cage)*, 2001]. Investigating the overlapping and even conflicting durational conditions—artistic, institutional, individual—that structure the ambulatory museum visitor's experience with these screen-reliant works, this chapter proposes that the generally individualized, exploratory duration of engaging gallery-based installations is central to the complexity of media installation both in terms of its critical leverage and its ideological function.

The final two chapters articulate the multiple spatial registers of the viewer's experience with media art environments and consider how artists have mobilized these spaces to critical effect. Chapter 4, "Be Here (and There) Now," analyzes the conceptual and physical spaces particular to viewing film and video screens configured as sculptural installations. Dominant theoretical models of the 1960s and 1970s tended to reject any use of representational illusionism and "cinematic" viewing as inherently uncritical—a proposition that continues to haunt current art criticism. The screens in media installations paradoxically reintroduce precisely the virtual, illusionist space that these earlier models had sought to evacuate but, crucially, without abandoning critical reflexivity. This chapter's rereading of key projects by VALIE EXPORT (*Ping Pong*, 1968) and Peter Campus (*Interface*, 1972) seeks to recuperate the critical subtlety of screen-based artworks that activate what one might call spectatorial doubleness: these works explore the complex nature of mediated vision by asking their viewers to be present in the real gallery space and the virtual screen space simultaneously.

"What Lies Ahead," the fifth and final chapter, analyzes transformations in the spatial conditions of viewing media art ushered in by the powerful yet amorphous networks associated with digital computer screens. Two prize-winning new media projects, Ken Goldberg's *The Telegarden* (1996) and Lynn Hershman's *The Difference Engine #3* (1995–98), serve as the central case studies. While the technical details of both of these multisited and teleactive digital works are far more complex than the media environments investigated in previous chapters, their concern with the spectator's relationship to the space(s) associated with viewing media screens is entirely consistent. This chapter concludes by posing an important question about new media installation art in general: are we, as spectators of these screen-reliant works, both here *and* there—or, perhaps more ominously, are we neither fully here *nor* there? Might the doubleness intrinsic to viewing screens in art installations not also be configured in such a way that spectators spread their attention across various technological interfaces while never being fully present in the experiential material world?

Building on the final chapter's discussion of digital screens, the Afterword offers some projections about the future of screen studies and gestures toward the political and ethical implications of the screen-based interactions that have become ubiquitous in art practice and in everyday life.

From movie screens to television sets, from video walls to PDAs, screens literally and figuratively stand between us, separating bodies and filtering communication between subjects. The Afterword restates an argument that runs throughout the text: there is a critical imperative to recognize the ways in which screens and conditions of screen-based viewing "matter" in both contemporary art and our digital everyday.

The underlying proposition of *Screens* is that present-day viewers are, quite literally, "screen subjects." With this in mind, the book analyzes how certain artworks (re)materialize the neglected circuit between bodies and screens and, in so doing, posit alternate engagements with contemporary media technologies. In what is arguably our "society of the screen," there can be no definitive external position from which to assess the conditions of media spectatorship. For this very reason questions about site and interface are crucial to the production of a truly critical practice and theory of screen-reliant installation art.

1. **Interface Matters** Screen-Reliant Installation Art

The brain is the screen . . . that is to say ourselves.

—GILLES DELEUZE, "An Interview with Gilles Deleuze"

Art critic and historian Michael Fried's groundbreaking 1967 essay, "Art and Objecthood," is best known as a studied rejection of minimalism, or, as Fried preferred to call it, "literalist" art. Fried recognized that this new genre, inasmuch as it compelled a durational viewing experience akin to theater, undermined both the medium specificity and the presumed instantaneousness of reception foundational to the Greenbergian/Friedan account of modernism. The impact of Fried's discerning analysis upon contemporary art history and criticism is incontestable. For the purposes of the present study, however, a little remarked upon footnote in this otherwise exhaustively analyzed article is especially revelatory. In it, Fried speculates that a close reading of the "phenomenology of the cinema" would reveal how film manages to escape the degraded relational quality that he believed was endemic to literalist art. "Exactly how the movies escape theater is a beautiful question," Fried muses. He goes on to suggest that cinema is not in danger of theatricality because, among other reasons, "the screen is not experienced as a kind of object existing, so to speak, in a specific physical relation to us."[1]

Fried's appreciation of a divide between the cinematic experience and that of minimalist sculpture was soon to be overthrown by the expanded field of art and media practices that emerged in the 1960s and 1970s. In the range of overlapping screen-reliant art practices variously known as structural film, expanded cinema, intermedia environments, moving-image or projected-image installation, and so on, the seemingly discrete boundaries between the cinematic and the sculptural were deliberately and provocatively muddied. Contesting the tenets of formalist modernism, artists as diverse

1

as VALIE EXPORT, Frank Gillette and Ira Schneider, Dan Graham, Joan Jonas, Anthony McCall, Marcel Broodthaers, Bruce Nauman, Peter Campus, Paul Sharits, and Michael Snow created evocative sculptures in which cinematic and electronic screens, defying Fried's analysis, are indeed "experienced as a kind of object existing . . . in a specific physical relation to us." Even before the inception of most film and video installations, then, Fried had instinctively recognized that the screen would be a threat to stable modernist categories should its conventionally overlooked objecthood be exposed (a threat he was keen to avoid). Working in the wake of minimalism, these artists did just that: they invited viewers to understand the screen — *as well as the site and experience of screen spectatorship* — as material.

Media screens made initial forays into art galleries as early as the late 1950s. Film and video screens served both as constitutive elements of happenings, performances, and expanded cinema events, created by artists such as Carolee Schneemann, Alan Kaprow, John Cage, Robert Whitman, and Robert Rauschenberg, and as art materials in their own right, such as the now quaintly anachronistic television sets assembled in Wolf Vostell's early media-critical work and in Nam June Paik's satirical video sculptures. However, the incorporation of mass media screens into art environments or installations in the mid-1960s marked a distinct shift of emphasis. In what I call screen-reliant installations, artists were newly concerned with the viewer–screen interface itself: the multifarious physical and conceptual points at which the observing subject meets the media object. Media objects and their viewing regimes were literally and figuratively put on display in these sculptural and experiential works of art.[2]

I use the term "screen-reliant" as opposed to "screen-based" to signal that a screen is a performative category. Almost anything — glass, architecture, three-dimensional objects, and so on — can function as a screen and thus as a connective interface to another (virtual) space.[3] Projected image installations have consistently revealed this ambiguous status — from Robert Whitman's 1964 *Shower,* in which a nude female bather is projected onto a real shower (complete with an actual running shower head), to, more recently, Michal Rover's 2003 *DataZone,* in which diminutive dancing figures are projected inside of what look like petri dishes mounted on tabletops. The screen, then, is a curiously ambivalent object — simultaneously a material entity and a virtual window; it is altogether an object which, when deployed in spatialized sculptural configurations, resists facile categorization.

Although the term "installation" was not widely used until the late 1970s, the issues associated with the expanded practices now commonly known as installation—considerations such as space, materials, embodiment, duration, site, and participation—offer the most relevant criteria for evaluating this variant of post-1960s artistic production. In many ways, minimalism and its critical legacy set the stage for these developments. Minimalism aspired to overthrow the spatial and temporal idealism associated with modernist sculpture, replacing it with a direct experiential encounter for the spectator in the "here and now" of the gallery space. By revealing the exhibition space as material, these influential artworks cleared the way for critical reflection on the physical and ideological constraints of the art gallery by process- and concept-based sculptural practices of the 1960s and 1970s.[4] In these innovative artworks, context and the contingent dynamics of spectatorship emerged as content.[5]

It was in this spirit that artists first created experiential works centered on media screens and sited within the specific institutional context of the visual arts. These hybrid artworks—positioned as they are midway between the cinematic and the sculptural—deliberately engaged the spatial parameters of the gallery, even as they rejected its typical spatial and representational modes. Regardless of the particular approach employed in a given work, these variegated screen-reliant environments are unified by the way in which they foreground the usually overlooked embodied interface between the viewing subject and the technological object.

By viewer-screen interface, I mean that which connects the viewer and the mechanisms for screening, including, at the most basic level, the film, camera, projector, and screen. Film apparatus theory in the 1970s marked the first rigorous attempt to combine an analysis of the materiality of cinema with its architectonic and ideological effects. Writers such as Jean-Louis Baudry, Jean-Louis Comolli, Christian Metz, Laura Mulvey, and Peter Wollen conceptualized cinema's institutional apparatus as a fixed relation between the film, projector, screen, and viewer.[6] Of equal importance, these critics and filmmakers, drawing heavily on psychoanalytic theory, offered the first theorization of the screen as both material surface and site for psychic projection.[7] Building from these concepts, while troubling the assumption of the viewing subject's enforced passivity vis-à-vis the apparatus, I consider this connective interface to be inclusive not only of the objects that make cinema possible, but also the psychological, phenomenological, and indeed ideological relationships between viewing subjects and media screens.[8] The viewer–screen connection is a site of radical inter-implication: it includes the projection screen and other material conditions of screening, but also encompasses sentient bodies and psychic desires, institutional codes, and discursive constructs.

Screens themselves have the curious status of functioning simultaneously as immaterial thresholds onto another space and time and as solid, material entities. The screen's objecthood, however, is typically overlooked in daily life: the conventional propensity is to look *through* media screens and not *at* them.[9] Although the screen is a notoriously slippery and ambivalent object, one that seems to outrun its shadow of materiality at every turn, its physical form shapes both its immediate space and its relationship to viewing subjects. In environmental media artworks, the screen object and the viewer's active, bodily experience with it can achieve a new centrality: the interface "matters" for media installation art. It matters in the sense that it constitutes an essential component of the artwork (the various dealings between spectators and the screen are structural to the work), but also because the body-screen interface is a phenomenal form in itself as well as a constitutive part of an embodied visual field.

That the relationship between the viewing subject and the screen "matters" is more than a perfunctory observation. It is a proposal for a theoretical model for assessing contemporary artistic production made with cinematic and electronic screens. Media installations, inasmuch as they are conceived and experienced as hybrid spatial and temporal art objects made with mass media screens, clearly exceed critical models that exclusively rely on outmoded theorizations of material specificity or of a single medium. Instead, these works necessitate detailed consideration of their institutional and discursive contexts. Even so, taking the screen and its connections to the viewer as an object of study is more fraught than it might sound. It has proved extremely intoxicating for critical theorists from Fredric Jameson to Paul Virilio to speculate about the screen's remarkable capacity to reorganize space and time.[10] Yet, in their preoccupation with the screen's more spectacular effects, these thinkers have taken little notice of the ways in which the screen's material configurations actively define its relationship to its site and to subjects.[11] A theory of screen-reliant art spectatorship should involve looking at what is depicted on the screen's surface and theorizing the media screen's time- and space-shifting effects to be sure, but it must also examine what these ambivalent material objects do and the various networks within which they do it.[12]

The operative conditions of screen-reliant art spectatorship will be carefully assessed in the chapters that follow. The task of the present chapter is to establish a working definition of screen-reliant installation (especially as distinct from other forms of experimental media production) and to theorize the critical relevance of these evocative art objects. Two early film environments that arguably take the relationship between viewers and screens as their very subject matter—Paul Sharits's *Soundstrip/Filmstrip* (1971–72) and Michael Snow's *Two Sides to Every Story* (1974)—are the principal case studies. Sharits and Snow are emblematic of a number of artists who began to mine the rich terrain between art and cinema in the 1960s and 1970s. While Fried's formalist modernism censured the deployment of the cinema screen as a literalist object, these artists created novel screen-reliant works that denied the terms of this criticism by holding objecthood and illusionism in tandem. Sharits and Snow merit special attention for the way they have self-consciously transgressed the boundaries between art and cinema and carefully distinguished among various filmic and artistic genres in both their writing and practice.

Film as Locational

"Cinema is occurring when one looks at screens, not through them," Paul Sharits proclaimed in 1974. "The space between screens is filled with actuality without recourse to phony densities."[13] Sharits was writing in reference to his art gallery–based film works that he called "locational," but what could a "cinema" of looking *at* screens be? In a 1976 essay, art historian Rosalind Krauss argues that works such as Sharits's locational pieces mark a turning point in filmic production because they incorporate the "real, physical environment" and "the viewer's actual experience between the parallel planes of screen and projector" into the work itself.[14] Whereas film's deep, illusionistic space had previously reigned supreme, commanding the viewer's undivided attention, in media installations such as Sharits's, multiple spaces began to compete for focal significance. As references to real world "actualities" supplanted film's alleged "phony densities," both the conditions of cinematic viewing and the screen itself suddenly became central to the artwork's meaning.

Sharits is best known as a leading figure in American structural film, a genre of experimental film that flourished in the 1960s and 1970s and whose primary interest was in documenting film's internal codes.[15] The filmmaker–artist turned toward making multiscreen locational environments/

installations in the early 1970s. In a 1974 manifesto, Sharits singled out four main imperatives for the development of the locational film works: (1) they must exist "in an open, free, public location"; (2) the form of presentation must not "prescribe a definite duration of respondent's observation (i.e., the respondent may enter and leave at any time)"; (3) the very structure of the composition must be "non-developmental" and offer "an immediately apprehensible system of elements"; and, finally, (4) the content of the work must "not disguise itself but rather make . . . a specimen of itself."[16] Examining how Sharits's prescriptions were emblematic of the era's optimism about the ostensibly progressive potential of gallery-based media work will be taken up in subsequent chapters. For the present argument, I'd like to draw attention only to this: in theorizing his locational installations as categorically distinct from his other filmic production (including structural film), Sharits went beyond formal attributes, concentrating instead on the new and oppositional viewing conditions presumably generated by the gallery-based works.

Given that experimental film and film installation share the same medium, how might we understand the nature of this alleged spectatorial transformation? Following Sharits's lead, one might begin by considering *T,O,U,C,H,I,N,G* (1968), one of his best-known structural films, side by side with *Soundstrip/Filmstrip* (1971–72), a nearly contemporaneous multi-screen installation.

T,O,U,C,H,I,N,G is a twelve-minute, 16 mm film composed of pure color shots and still images arranged into all sorts of configurations that pulsate at irregular, spastic intervals when projected.[17] The film is dedicated to and stars the poet David Franks. Interspersed throughout the film's discordant flashing color frames, Franks appears poised to cut off his own tongue with scissors while he obsessively repeats the word "destroy" in an urgent rhythmic stutter. Compounding the overall perceptual overload generated by the alternating color and achromatic flashes, the sound also "flickers": Franks's on/off pulsing voice renders his recurring pronouncement extremely indistinct as his meditative repetition of "destroy" causes it to fold back onto itself, generating alternate words ("history"/"the story"/"this story"/"this drawing," etc.). Nonetheless, the optical dimension of the audience's experience with *T,O,U,C,H,I,N,G* remains primary. To use Sharits's words, so-called flicker films constitute a form of "neural transmission" in which "the retina screen is a target."[18] When viewed in a darkened theater, the intensity of the projected color bursts seems to emanate aggressively from the screen itself, pushing the limits of the viewer's perceptual

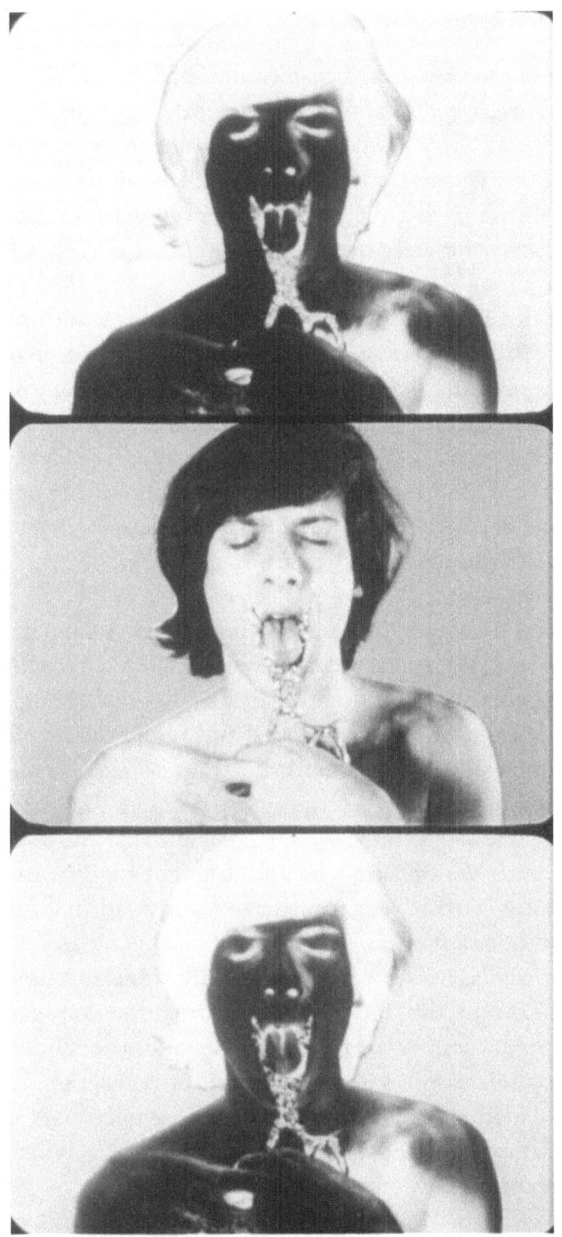

Paul Sharits, *T,O,U,C,H,I,N,G,* 1968. Film still from 12-minute, 16 mm "flicker film" composed of pure color shots and still images arranged into varied configurations that pulsate at irregular, spastic intervals when projected. Courtesy of Anthology Film Archives. All rights reserved. Copyright Christopher Sharits.

capabilities and generating hallucinatory after-images (what P. Adams Sitney has memorably referred to as the "basic apocalypse of the flicker").[19] Like many flicker films, *T,O,U,C,H,I,N,G* constitutes an aggressive opticality, a sort of retina-searing op art whose lingering visual effects momentarily prohibit viewers from resting their weary eyes even when closed. Captive in their theater seats, audience members must brace themselves for the film's twelve-minute-long visual assault.[20]

Created three years later, *Soundstrip/Filmstrip* is made up of four film projectors encased within large boxes positioned side by side in the middle of a partially illuminated gallery space measuring approximately 30 by 36 feet. Each of the four machines simultaneously projects an abstract color film of parallel stripes onto the opposite wall, which serves as a Cinemascope-esque screen. The four films are projected sideways and abutting one another in a continuous horizontal band, which has the effect of giving viewers the immediate (but mistaken) impression that they are seeing a single film projected sideways (four frames of which are visible to the viewer at any one time). A sound track of a dispassionate male voice stammering nearly indecipherable word fragments accompanies each film: a cacophony of what *initially* seems to be whispered, disjunctive nonsense. While the film technically has a fixed length, both the visual and auditory elements are played on a continuous loop so that the work has no evident beginning or end.

From these abbreviated descriptions of *T,O,U,C,H,I,N,G* and *Soundstrip/Filmstrip* one might provisionally conclude that the two pieces have more in common than Sharits's manifesto might suggest. After all, these films are clearly "artistic" experiments—(nearly) abstract, nonnarrative works that, although they use film, fall well outside the realm of what one typically thinks of as mainstream cinema. Both works unambiguously seek to trouble the perspectival illusionism that structures dominant cinematic forms, whether by emphasizing the function and materiality of film or by drawing attention to the subjective nature of perception itself. To this end, they ask their audiences to consider similar questions: What does it mean to be denied entry into the film's illusionist space? What are the constitutive elements in how one experiences a film?

Despite the similarities between the two works, it is important to distinguish among these "alternative" uses of film. The first and most obvious difference is not formal but rather institutional: Sharits's locational works were explicitly created for the distinctive context/site of an art gallery, not for a darkened cinema. The second (though related) difference is experi-

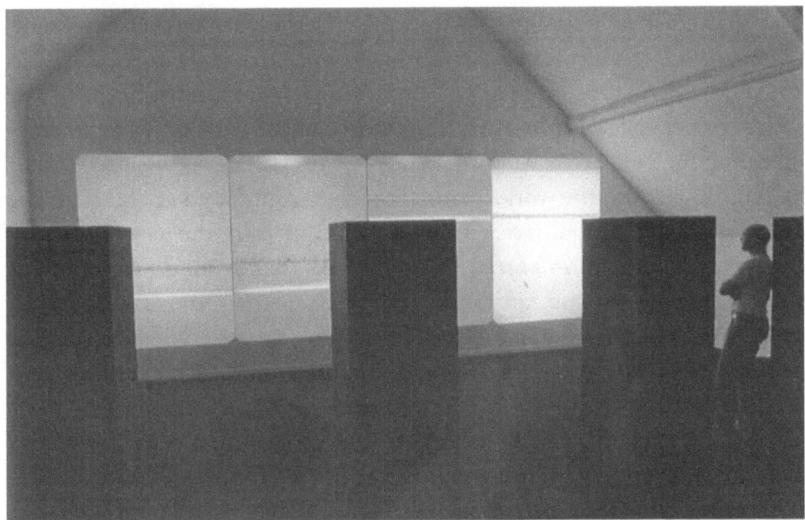

Paul Sharits, *Soundstrip/Filmstrip*, 1971–72. Installation view
from "Paul Sharits: Figment" exhibition at Espace Gantner,
France, 2007. Four projectors on black pedestals simultaneously
emit four separate but related films onto a single wall/screen
in what the artist refers to as a "locational" exhibition.
Copyright Christopher Sharits.

ential. While unconventional in its visual content, *T,O,U,C,H,I,N,G* is presented and experienced in a theatrical, cinematic fashion: the audience is separated from the (single) screen in a darkened enclosure in which the spectator's physical engagement with the film and the screening space is conspicuously limited. (This despite the viewer's apparent *physiological* and ocular engagement with the work due to its startlingly harsh, headache-inducing flicker effect.) Viewers come into contact with *Soundstrip/Filmstrip* in a dim (not dark) room in which the audience is expected to remain standing. Its mural-sized representations envelop an entire wall of the exhibition space and require spectators to spread their attention across four separate sets of projected images to take in the work. While audience members watching *T,O,U,C,H,I,N,G* are expected to remain stationary, viewers of *Soundstrip/Filmstrip*—whether they try to inch inconspicuously behind the illuminated imagery or fumble their way through the obstacle course of life-size projector boxes whirring like so many kinetic sculptures—are encouraged, and in fact required, to move physically through the exhibition space.

Sharits's structural film lasts for twelve (sometimes excruciating) minutes, whereas the locational installation is screened, as Sharits puts it, in an "ongoing, no beginning or ending, constantly variational form."[21] The viewer's experience with *Soundstrip/Filmstrip* is of an open-ended, exploratory duration: the peripatetic viewer is allowed to determine the length of his or her encounter with the work. Though the time committed to observing the installation will naturally vary from person to person, the viewer's experience with *Soundstrip/Filmstrip*, like the work itself, is meant to unfold in time and space. As spectators progress through the room, taking in the piece from various sites (and *only* if they do so), they eventually are able to decipher the relationships between the disparate moving image and sound fragments.

Sharits's viewer's initial confusion when confronted with *Soundstrip/Filmstrip*'s seemingly random sound track is rectified once he or she explores the work from various spatial points. Slowly negotiating their way through the film as an entire spatial environment, spectators figure out that the sound snakes from right to left and that the ostensibly indecipherable word fragments are in fact each constituent parts of a single word: "miscellaneous" (a word evocative of the work's outwardly unrelated elements that collectively generate the piece's meaning). Likewise, close scrutiny of the relationship between the projectors, images, and the wall-cum-screen reveals that each of the slightly overlapping moving film frames is a separate projection.[22] In this way, the viewer's active participation in the exhibition space serves to underscore the embodied and material conditions of film viewing.

Screen-reliant installation artworks such as *Filmstrip/Soundstrip* self-reflexively foreground the viewer-screen interface in a way that tends not to occur in mainstream narrative cinema or even in experimental film.[23] Film in Sharits's locational environments/installations is exposed as a material process and presented as an environment: film is considered to be a *space*. This space is made up of immaterial projected images but also the physical media apparatus; the screen, film, and projectors emerge as sculptural objects in their own right. Moreover, contrary to conventional cinematic viewing configurations, this filmic space is open to, even contingent upon, the mobile viewer's active phenomenological engagement in space and time, firmly situating Sharits's work within the critical ambitions of contemporary art discourse and in relationship to minimalism's critical lineage in particular.

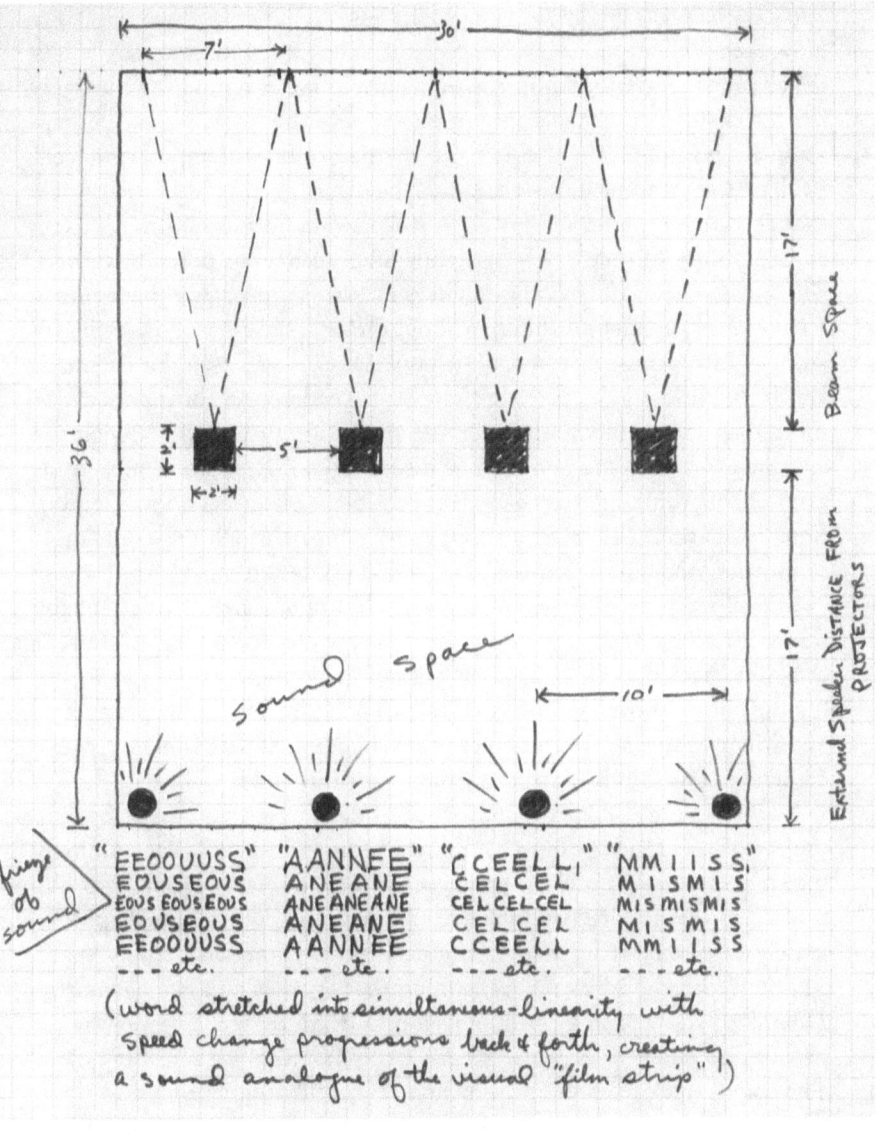

Paul Sharits, *Soundstrip/Filmstrip*, 1971–72. Artist's diagram indicating the artist's conception of how to install the work's sound, image, and object elements in relationship to the gallery space. Copyright Christopher Sharits.

More Than Meets the Eye

How the viewer experiences the spectator-screen interface in screen-reliant installations like *Soundstrip/Filmstrip* is just as meaningful as the imagery the screens depict. Equally important, however, these works are perhaps uniquely positioned to enable us to consider our contemporary screen-mediated communications critically: they can serve as heuristic devices that allow us to better understand the electronic mediations that inform contemporary subjectivity (or, perhaps more accurately, postsubjectivity). Theorist John Rajchman looks to Gilles Deleuze's provocative theorizing in *Cinema 2* as a model for thinking about the larger history of image instal-lation. "In making such invention possible, *dispositifs* like the cinematic are distinguished as something more than 'media' or technical supports, more than means of transmitting and receiving information," Rajchman explains. "They are, rather, ways of disposing of our senses in such a way as to enable thinking, to make ideas possible."[24] Michael Snow's seminal film installation *Two Sides to Every Story* (1974), which self-consciously scrutinizes modes of screen-mediated vision inside and outside the gallery's "white cube," is exemplary in this regard: it proposes new ways to inhabit screen interfaces and, in so doing, "makes new ideas possible." Examining this multifaceted work in detail will establish a critical lexicon for analyz-ing the points of overlap in post-1960s art and film and media production and will provide an introduction to the salient issues pertaining to screen-based spectatorship that structure the rest of this book.

Two Sides to Every Story consists of two analogous 16 mm color films projected synchronously onto both sides of a smooth, rectangular aluminum screen suspended in mid-air at the center of a dimly lit room. Two film projectors are mounted on top of black pedestals and positioned approxi-mately forty feet apart at opposite ends of the otherwise empty space. Although the films are each eight minutes long, they are, like *Soundstrip/Filmstrip*, projected in a continuous loop, effectively granting viewers the privilege to enter or leave the gallery at any point in the screening cycle. The sound track features ambient noise from the filming process—foot-steps, equipment movements, gentle rain—as well as Snow's voice direct-ing the action, which, depending on which side the viewer is focusing on, may or may not reconcile with what is depicted on the screen. That is, one is either positioned as a cinematic viewer, looking *into* the screen's deep space to see the story illustrated within, or is displaced, afforded an unexpected "behind the scenes" view of the filming process, comparable

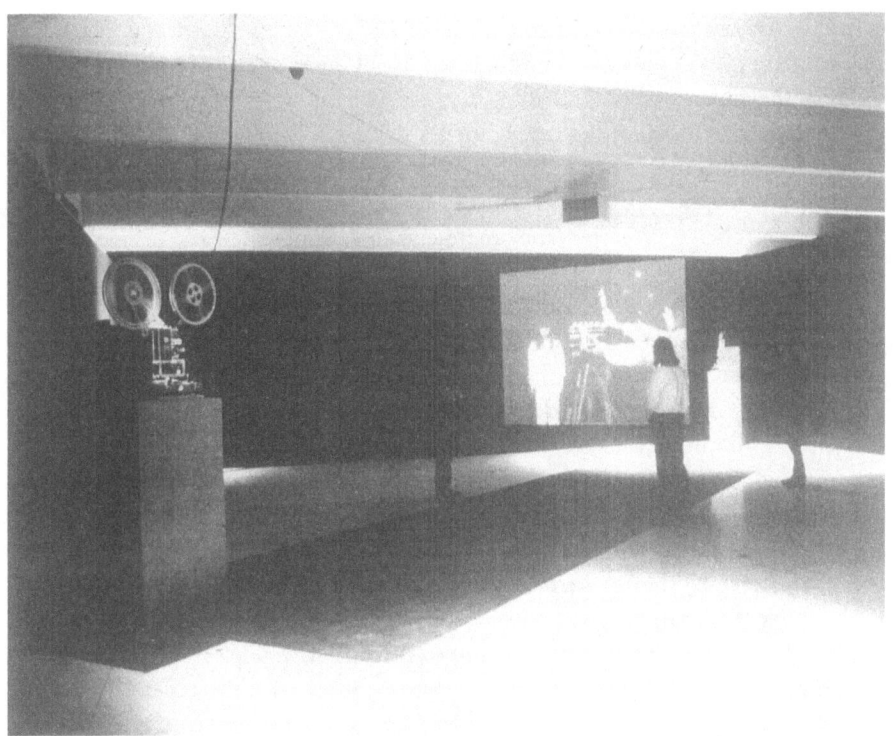

Michael Snow, *Two Sides to Every Story*, 1974. Installation view from "Projected Images" exhibition at the Walker Art Center, Minneapolis, 1974. This complex 8-minute work consists of two synchronized 16 mm films, color, and sound, projected continuously on two sides of an aluminum screen. Copyright Michael Snow.

to that of the director himself. (Viewers will in fact have both experiences at some point, although never both at once.)

What is not immediately obvious is that the projection situation discloses the way in which the work was originally shot. The two *projectors* stand forty feet apart from each other in the gallery, duplicating the way in which the two *cameras* were set up on either side of the original filming location. For the gallery installation, Snow substitutes the cameras with the projectors, neatly transposing the entire shooting/production space into the viewing/installation space. Furthermore, because the cameras captured the action at the center of the room from opposing corners, each film also records the camera, tripod, and camera operator stationed opposite. In this way, the two films jointly chronicle their own production.

Throughout their experience with *Two Sides to Every Story,* spectators continually see (and hear) the undisguised list of ingredients required for staging the film's artifice, including the artist/director himself, who appears seated next to one of the camera operators.

The spectator's perambulation between both sides of the (literally) silver screen allows him or her to ascertain that although there are two separate films being projected, they represent dual, nonhierarchical perspectives of a single, seemingly mundane event. The subject matter is outwardly uninspiring—a young, casually dressed woman makes a series of movements while repeatedly walking between one camera operator and another situated at opposite sides of a room, presumably the artist's studio. Within moments, however, this deceptively simple narrative quickly draws the viewer into numerous conceptual conundrums. Following Snow's audible directions, the protagonist demonstrates that there is some kind of object in the center of the shooting space. She does this by pressing her hands against a nearly invisible, thin, transparent plastic sheet and subsequently coating its see-though surface with green spray paint.

Next, a man enters the scene, cuts the green plastic through the center, and walks through the opening to the opposite side. The woman follows him and the plastic sheet is removed. Snow then directs the woman to walk back and forth between the cameras carrying a rectangular mat board colored blue on one side and yellow on the other. Her movements with the dual-colored cards are echoed at irregular intervals by the actions of the two camera operators who Snow directs to cover the camera lenses with blue and yellow (or both) translucent plastic filters. Finally, the woman returns to the center and extends her hands *as if* pressing against a surface, figuratively remaking the plastic sheet qua screen, which symbolically links the immaterial image of the plastic sheet to the real aluminum film screen/projection plane in the installation.

In spite of this, it is not the projected images or the narrative alone that grabs and holds the viewer's interest. Entering the darkened gallery, one encounters Snow's illuminated metal screen that seems to hover in midair. Cheekily renouncing its role as wallflower, refusing to assume its conventional, discrete placement on or near a wall, the screen asserts itself as a sculptural object. Instead of obediently fading into the background at the moment of the viewing encounter, Snow's dual-sided projection surface (re)materializes in the exhibition space. Despite its apparent thinness (indeed, Snow's emaciated slice of aluminum seems almost to disappear when the spectator views it from the edges instead of head-on), the screen physically and symbolically cleaves the room in two, obliging viewers to observe the work from one side or the other if they hope to take in the projected images (which, of course, they do).

The emphatic objecthood of the screen is an indispensable foil to expose what Snow has called the radical nonmateriality of the filmic image. He writes: "Film itself—what one sees when a film is projected—is almost nonexistent *matière* on a flat surface. The fact that the image, which can contain such convincing representations of depth, is truly very, very thin is for me a poignant aspect of projected-light work. I believe that the actual thin, physical manifestation which is the image is as important in artworks as what the image represents." Ultimately, however, *Two Sides to Every Story* necessitates a visual skepticism in its viewers as they appreciate both the "thinness" of the filmic image and the convincing illusion of depth at the same time.[25] The slim two-sided projection surface is pivotal in structuring this experience: cinematic illusionism is supported or deconstructed depending on one's physical placement and point of view.

Faced with this unusual configuration, Snow's spectators must negotiate an improvised path between the two sides to probe the correlation between the dual views. Like Sharits's "locational" works, the organizing logic of Snow's installation only becomes apparent over time, through the viewer's ambulation and observation from a range of perspectives. And yet, for all of the effort expended in the viewer's awkward, unchoreographed dance between dueling sides of *Two Sides to Every Story*'s projection plane, he or she will never have the satisfaction or closure of seeing everything all at once. Mastery of the visual material remains perpetually just out of reach.

"Events take time. Events take place," Snow observed in *Artforum* in 1971. "In relation to events one can only be a participant or a spectator or," he is quick to add, "both."[26] As if offering a consolation prize to his stymied would-be film viewers as they repeatedly pace between both faces of the illuminated silver plane, Snow encourages them to conceptualize themselves in two additional roles. Having insistently established that there are indeed two sides to every screen, Snow extends the idea, exposing how there is also a duality in screen-mediated spectatorship. On the one hand, the viewer's movements echo the protagonist's methodical pacing, so that the spectator is symbolically remade into the film's subject and asked to identify with the female performer, who patiently obeys the director's rather monotonous instructions. On the other hand, the work's visitors perform the same function as the film cameras, their role as mediators or translators of the work's meaning echoing the camera's mediation. While

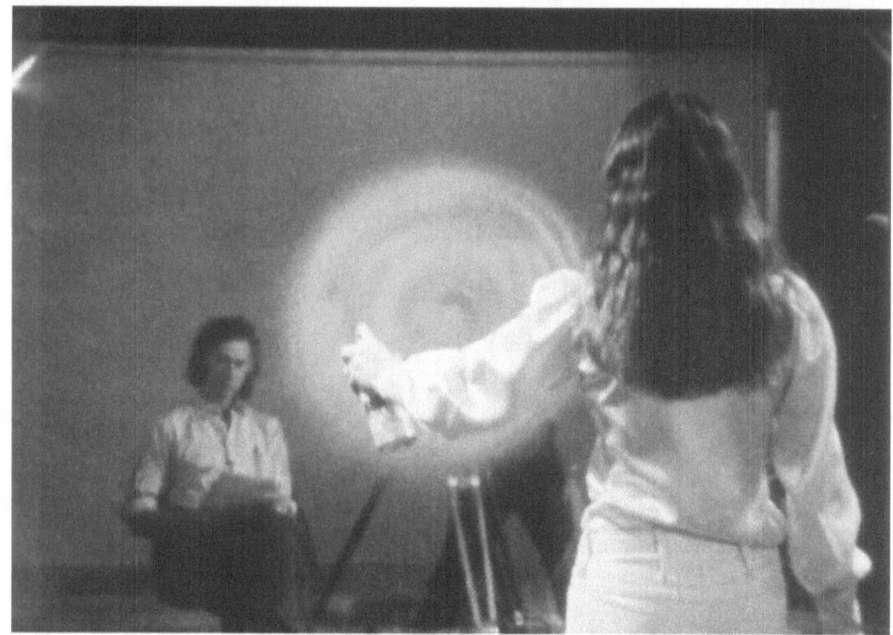

Michael Snow, *Two Sides to Every Story*, 1974. Recto and
verso views of the moving imagery projected simultaneously
onto both sides of the installation's two-sided screen.
Copyright Michael Snow.

spectators are scrupulously forbidden visual mastery, they are intellectually
rewarded for ruminating on the implications of their screen-mediated
viewing experience, one that is understood to be both passive and active.

Writing in 1974, critic Regina Cornwell praised Snow's installation
for the way in which its screen makes the spectator conscious of the space
of the event, as opposed to its normative function as a "'window to the
world' in order that we may lose ourselves."[27] This assessment maps neatly
onto the dominant approaches to media art criticism of the period.[28]
Informed by a curious amalgamation of minimalism's phenomenological
legacy, postminimalism's explorations of process and institutional critique,
and the ideological critiques of film and media theory that sought to lib-
erate the spectator–subject by revealing the media apparatus, these models
rejected any use of representational illusionism and "cinematic" viewing as
inherently passive and therefore uncritical. What Cornwell intuits but
never fully articulates is how *Two Sides to Every Story* turns this equation
on its head. Snow's installation implicitly reintroduces precisely the virtual,

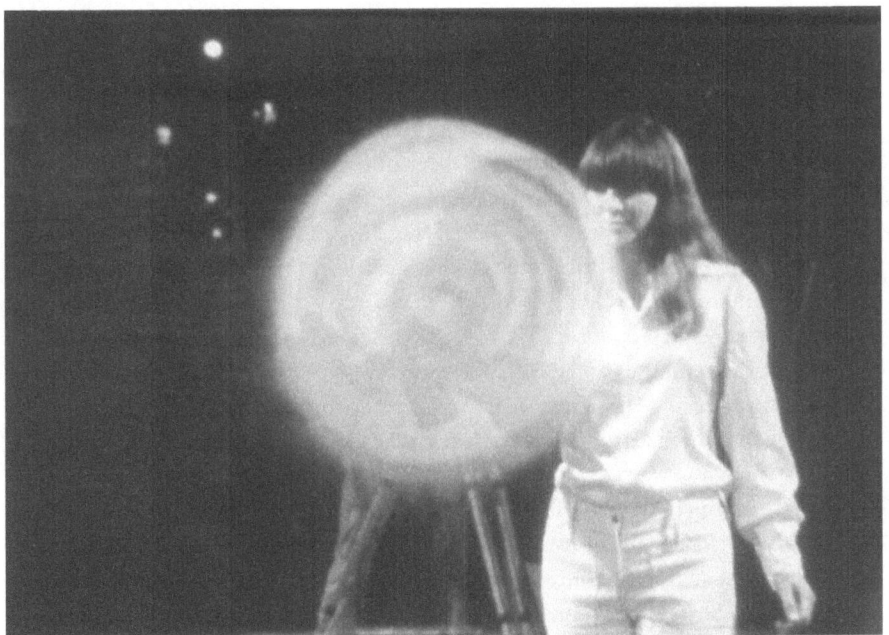

illusionist space that these other critical models had sought to evacuate without, however, abandoning critical reflexivity.

Many (but by no means all) screen-reliant installations are less concerned with purely artistic/sculptural or filmic/cinematic concerns than they are with the nature of contemporary visuality as pertains to screen spectatorship and with the body-screen interface in particular. As film critic Dominique Païni astutely observes about *Two Sides to Every Story,* "It is the screen, *essentially* the screen, more than an abstract filmic material, which is Snow's burden."[29] Submitting a film screen as part of an art gallery installation, Snow's work effectively generates a hybrid between painting's representational illusionism and sculpture's three-dimensional materiality.[30] Although irreducible to either role, the film screen is exposed as both a cipher—a (non)site for illusionist content—*and* an object to reckon with in its own right. However much Snow might be preoccupied with what Sharits would call screen-based "actualities," *Two Sides to Every Story* does not eradicate the screen's inherent "phony densities." Instead, the work reveals an apparent paradox of media installation spectatorship: this mode of viewing is simultaneously material (the viewer's phenomenological engagement with actual objects in real time and space) and immaterial (the viewer's metaphorical projection into virtual times and spaces).

Snow has commented upon the nature of this doubleness. In an unpublished interview with Cornwell, Snow remarked that he wasn't so much working *against* illusory deep space in film as he was using "the 'belief' in it along with the 'fact of flatness' and having it both ways."[31] *Two Sides to Every Story* describes an unresolved tension between the fact of the film screen's flatness and the mass media viewer's desire for, and habituation to, the illusory deep spaces it displays. To this end the work deconstructs filmic conventions within an art gallery setting.[32] Snow appears to deliberately take aim at Hollywood-style continuity editing, for example, by exposing the way in which viewers unconsciously make up for the apparent ruptures inherent in the classic shot/reverse shot technique.[33]

In observing *Two Sides to Every Story* spectators are incontrovertibly responsive to the projection surface's material form, inasmuch as it dictates their awkward circumnavigation. Nevertheless, audience members remain compelled by the screen's illusory representational spaces. In watching the onscreen narrative unfold, Snow's viewers are fully convinced of the virtual window's "interior" space even while they are unremittingly reminded of its staged constructedness, confronted with its logical impossibility. *Two Sides to Every Story*, as its very title insinuates, highlights the doubleness structural both to the media screen and to the viewer's experience with it inside the art gallery. In so doing, the artist plays with a structural characteristic of much conventional mass media spectatorship, in which viewers are habitually asked to see "into" cinematic and electronic screen spaces without paying particular attention to the media object's material form or its relationship to its site.

Having It Both Ways

The redeployment of screens in art installations thus potentially constitutes a powerful interrogation of the ideological and phenomenological properties of media screens themselves. In bringing the screen-based apparatus to the center of attention and, in this manner, positioning the viewer–screen interface and screen spectatorship itself as content, media artworks such as Sharits's and Snow's reflexively explore the complex nature of screen-mediated vision. It is a truism that in everyday life we spend countless hours looking into screens and not at them. When perfectly functional in daily life, film, video, and computer screens often seem to disappear. By asking us to consider the implications of this condition, artists such as Sharits and Snow propose that screens and our relationship to them "matter."

The interface conditions between viewers and screens *always* matter, of course, however much they may tend to escape notice in everyday life. In his essay "Leaving the Movie Theater," Roland Barthes identifies a potentially productive way of experiencing mainstream cinema: "by letting oneself be fascinated twice over, by the image and its surroundings—as if I had two bodies at the same time: a narcissistic body which gazes, lost, into the engulfing mirror, and a perverse body, ready to fetishize not the image but precisely what exceeds it: the texture of the sound, the hall, the darkness, the obscure mass of the other bodies."[34] Screen-reliant installations are therefore exemplary to the extent that they make viewers reflexively aware of this condition, persuasively (and persistently) reminding them of the necessarily embodied and material nature of all media viewing.[35] Chapter 2 will take up the peculiar model of screen-directed spectator participation proposed in a series of influential closed-circuit video installations by Frank Gillette and Ira Schneider, Bruce Nauman, and Dan Graham. Like the works by Sharits and Snow, these projects afford us a position from which to analyze the nature of screen spectatorship. In so doing, they also put forth a rather unsettling proposition: that we are, quite literally, screen subjects—largely defined by our daily interactions mediated through a range of screen-based technological devices.

2. **Body and Screen** The Architecture of Screen Spectatorship

Frank Gillette and Ira Schneider's *Wipe Cycle* (1969) greets viewers with flickering black-and-white electronic images that rotate through a grid of nine stacked televisions. Commonly lauded as the first work in the field of video installation, *Wipe Cycle* also numbers among the first to incorporate live feedback by employing closed-circuit video technology. The television sets are arranged in rows of three—an illuminated tic-tac-toe board displaying continuously shifting arrangements of live and prerecorded footage interspersed with images of the work's viewers themselves. Observers stand entranced before the glowing sculptural environment, studying the intricate shifting combinations of pictures, including their own likenesses. Gray light impulses, or "wipe cycles," periodically brush across the stacked surfaces, temporarily canceling all imagery. This seemingly haphazard visual display instead follows a detailed script: live playback depicting the viewers' images always appears in the center monitor, for instance, while the videotapes and television feed wander between bordering screens in one of four programming sequences interspersed with time delays of between eight and sixteen seconds. In the art critic's rush to examine the various scenarios played out on the multiple monitors, however, one might neglect a more basic question: how, precisely, do viewers look at screen-reliant sculptures?

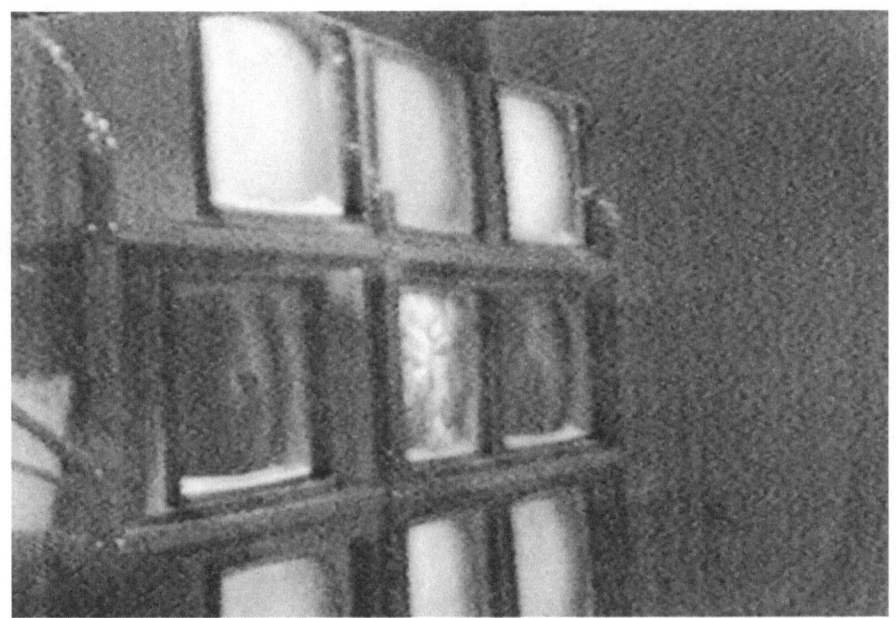

Frank Gillette and Ira Schneider, *Wipe Cycle,* 1969. Installation view from "TV as a Creative Medium" exhibition at the Howard Wise Gallery, New York, 1969. This side view emphasizes the objecthood of the screens that compose the closed-circuit video environment. Courtesy of Frank Gillette and Ira Schneider.

How might the terms of engaging media installations differ (or not) from observing other art objects?

The moving images and illuminated surfaces of screen-reliant works provoke a different kind of attention from other art objects, both psychologically and physiologically. On the most basic level, moving and illuminated imagery insistently solicits the observer's gaze and in so doing disciplines his or her body. Here I am less concerned with distinctions of the degree of attention various media screens presumably demand—such as the "gaze" conventionally associated with cinematic viewing, in pointed contrast to the "glance" supposedly characteristic of television viewing—than with the fact that illuminated media screens tend to immediately draw the spectator's attention in any context, if only for an instant.[1] Attention, observes art historian Jonathan Crary in his *Suspensions of Perception,* is the feature of perception that enables subjects to focus on portions of their surroundings and delay or neglect the remainder. The viewer's shifting attentive

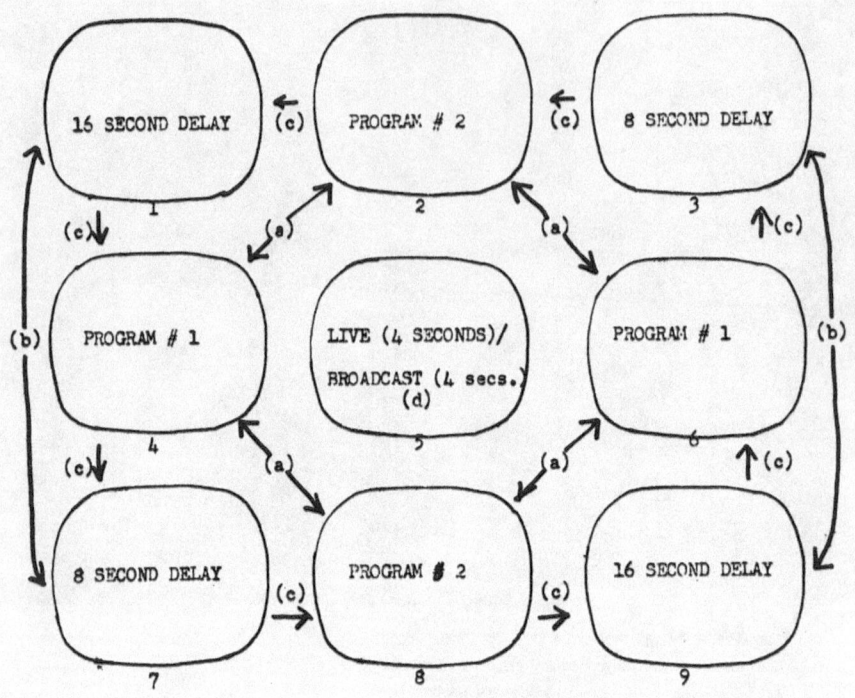

CYCLE (a)   Monitors 2, 4, 6 and 8: Programmed change cycle, Program No. 1 alternating every eight seconds with Program No. 2.

CYCLE (b)   Monitors 1, 3, 7 and 9: Delay change cycle, Nos. 1 and 7 and 3 and 9 alternating (exchanging) every four seconds.

CYCLE (c)   Monitors 1, 2, 3, 4, 6, 7, 8 and 9: Wipe cycle, grey "light" pulse, moving counterclockwise every two seconds.

CYCLE (d)   Monitor 5: Live cycle, four seconds of live feedback alternating with four seconds of broadcast television.

Frank Gillette and Ira Schneider, *Wipe Cycle*, 1969. Artist's diagram of the installation's complex video-programming cycles. Courtesy of Frank Gillette and Ira Schneider.

conduct with screen-based technologies, then, has weighty consequences for media art spectatorship.

Although this chapter will investigate the cultural foundations for this behavior—why and how viewers focus on media screens, whether inside or outside of the art gallery—physiological explanations are equally noteworthy. Scientist Christof Koch, for example, in an important neurobiological study of consciousness, explains how the viewer's focus on certain objects is essentially involuntary. "Some things don't need focal attention to be noticed. They are conspicuous by virtue of intrinsic attributes relative to their surroundings," he writes. "These salient objects rapidly, transiently, and automatically attract attention." Screens, he points out, aggressively and inexorably claim a certain amount of concentration. Tellingly, the ubiquitous video screen is Koch's first concrete example: "It takes willful effort to avoid glancing at the moving images on the TV placed above the bar in a saloon."[2] Koch's account is helpful in explaining the observer's obedient posture in front of flickering images such as those in *Wipe Cycle,* even if, as rehearsed in the previous chapter, the viewer's experience with screens employed in sculptural installations can be considerably more complex. As we shift from the saloon to the salon, Koch's point about how certain salient objects unavoidably influence viewing subjects remains pivotally important for theorizing the operative conditions of screen-based art spectatorship.

Made You Look

The prevailing trends of media installation art criticism that seek to account for the role of the viewer can be divided essentially into two groups. On the one hand, critics celebrate the supposed spectatorial empowerment and liberation associated with audience participation (more recently described as "interactivity"). On the other hand, in an apparent contradiction, scholars condemn the observer's allegedly passive and uncritical experience observing mass media screens as reflective of the technological structures and control mechanisms of late capitalism.[3] It is not so much the active participation and/or passive viewing associated with these works that requires critical exploration, however, but rather the multifaceted and ambivalent relationship between a self-consciously embodied spectatorship and the disciplinary aspects of screen-based visuality. While critical accounts written since 2005 or so have developed more nuanced theories of attentive regulation and control as potential sites of cultural contestation,[4] the majority of these critiques also fundamentally fail to appreciate what one might call media installation's "architecture of spectatorship": the defining role of the screen apparatus in managing the interactions between viewing subjects and media objects.[5]

Any artwork proffering the seductive glow of an illuminated screen is reasonably entitled to the schoolyard taunt "made you look." Closed-circuit video installations such as *Wipe Cycle,* however, make you look even closer—because *you* are literally in the picture. "The most important function of *Wipe Cycle,*" recalls Schneider, "was to integrate the audience into the information."[6] For Schneider, the work's live feedback system disrupts normative television viewing by integrating the viewer's image into what is typically considered to be a one-way flow of information. Art historian David Joselit observes how works such as *Wipe Cycle,* although sited in the relatively controlled environment of the gallery, proved generative for other forms of video activism in the 1970s; guerrilla television's production of politically engaged documentaries on cable, for example, shared the aspiration for what Gillette describes as "a symbiotic feedback between receiving and broadcasting."[7] While Joselit's larger argument about video experimentation will be taken up in what follows, for now it suffices to note that these influential early video installations also offer a particularly useful way to understand the disciplinary and attention aspects of screen-based art spectatorship. By focusing on these pioneering examples, in which viewers' bodies are unambiguously implicated in the work via feedback, one can extrapolate the ways in which media art environments impose particular physical arrangements upon their audiences in less obvious cases. Thus, while the early video installations of the late 1960s and early 1970s offer the best examples, the mode of spectatorship they promote persists in much current media art production as well.

Through case studies of seminal video art projects, including Bruce Nauman's corridor pieces created between 1969 and 1972, and Dan Graham's *Present Continuous Past(s)* (1974), this chapter scrutinizes not only the ways in which media objects and their customary viewing regimes actively define the relationship between bodies and screens, but also how certain closed-circuit video works intentionally underscore the coercive nature of screen-based viewing. That is, through an assortment of techniques, such as varying the arrangement of cameras and monitors, combining live and prerecorded feedback, inverting viewers' images, divorcing cameras from their monitors, and introducing time delays, these artworks demonstrate how the viewing regimes associated with technological apparatuses assert precise kinesthetic and psychic effects upon their audiences. This chapter proposes that certain video installations can generate critical moments of rupture from within established forms and techniques of screen-based control: while these screen-reliant works oblige attention and discipline viewers' bodies, the subjective effects of those requirements are remarkably unfixed.

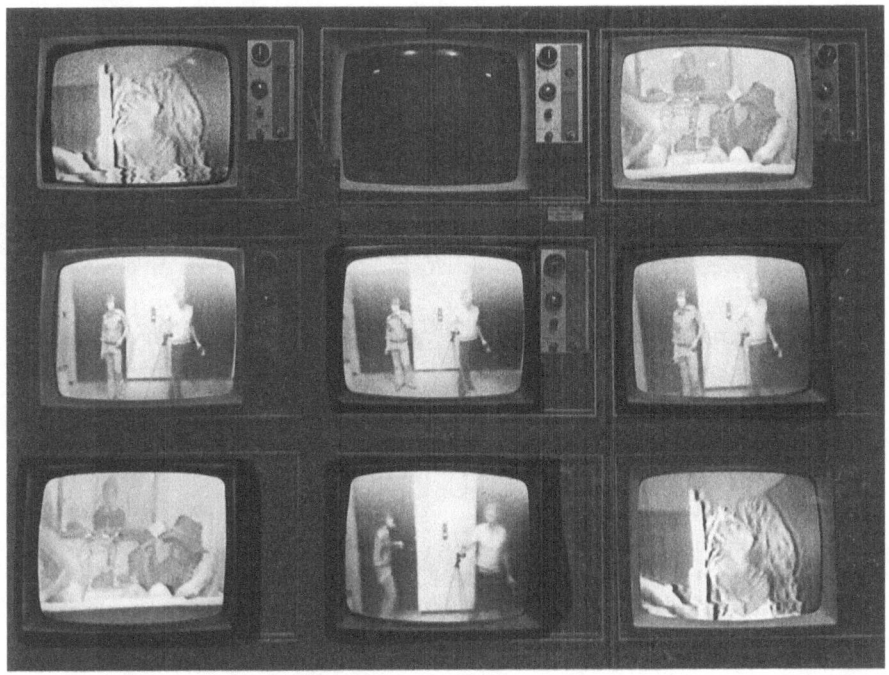

Frank Gillette and Ira Schneider, *Wipe Cycle*, 1969. Installation
view from "TV as a Creative Medium" exhibition at the Howard
Wise Gallery, New York, 1969. This view demonstrates how
images of the viewers observing the work are captured by
closed-circuit cameras and represented in the center and
bottom screens. Courtesy of Frank Gillette and Ira Schneider.

Get in Line: Bruce Nauman's Video Corridors

Considerations of "active" or participatory spectatorship have been inti-
mately related to the discourse surrounding installation art since its inception. Indeed, the viewer's involvement with the work is often taken to be
the defining feature of the art form. In her 2000 monograph on installation art, art historian and curator Julie Reiss emphasizes that "the spectator is in some way regarded as integral to the completion of the work" and
goes so far as to propose that "the essence of installation art *is* spectator
participation."[8] Contemporary art practice and criticism, profoundly in-
fluenced by Marxist critiques of alienation, phenomenological critiques of
Cartesianism, and poststructuralist critiques of authorship, conventionally
understands the spectator's active participation to be progressive for purportedly engendering an empowered, critically aware viewing subject. Installation

artworks are thus habitually positioned alongside radical politics and progressive aesthetics for the way in which they are thought to counteract passive, resigned viewing by providing an experiential encounter for the spectator. In sum, the critical discourse surrounding this art form pits active, open-ended reception (especially associated with Brecht's materialist and collectivist notion of aesthetic reception) against passive consumption.

The automatic praise of audience participation obscures an inconsistency, however.[9] While installation art's bid for the spectator's involvement is routinely understood to constitute an open-ended invitation that constructs a critically aware viewer, the "invitation" runs the risk of demanding a predetermined and even compulsory response.[10] Put differently, the viewer's presumably open-ended participatory experience with a given work is instead imposed by the very art form of installation; by necessitating active spectator involvement, whether implicitly or explicitly, installation artworks may simultaneously constitute environments of controlled passive response. While the way in which viewer participation emerges as a form of submission has recently begun to be addressed in regard to installation in general, works made with screen-based technologies have received less scrutiny.

Nowhere are the disciplinary aspects of viewing screens more apparent than in Nauman's video corridor installations. These celebrated sculptures are part of the artist's larger collection of corridor works—which incorporated materials as diverse as neon, mirrors, fans, and so on—primarily created between 1969 and 1972. Regardless of the various media introduced in each work, all of the sculptures feature a corridor or corridorlike structure whose domineering spatial presence closely restricts the audience's viewing experience.[11] The series began with *Performance Corridor* (1969), a repurposed studio prop that consists simply of two wallboard dividers mounted parallel to each other to form a long, twenty-inch-wide passageway. Confronted by this almost impossibly narrow shaft, museum visitors must enter the makeshift corridor's dim, claustrophobic space to take in the piece. In this case, the physical architecture (the wallboard panels) sharply directs the spectators' bodies. In Nauman's corridors made with video, however, the bullying of built structures takes a backseat to screen-based manipulation.[12]

Live-Taped Video Corridor (1970), like the original *Performance Corridor*, features a long and narrow wallboard construction. It is distinguished from the first work by the inclusion of a camera (inconspicuously mounted at the top of the corridor near its entrance) and two monitors stacked one on top of the other on the floor in front of the far wall. The piggybacked

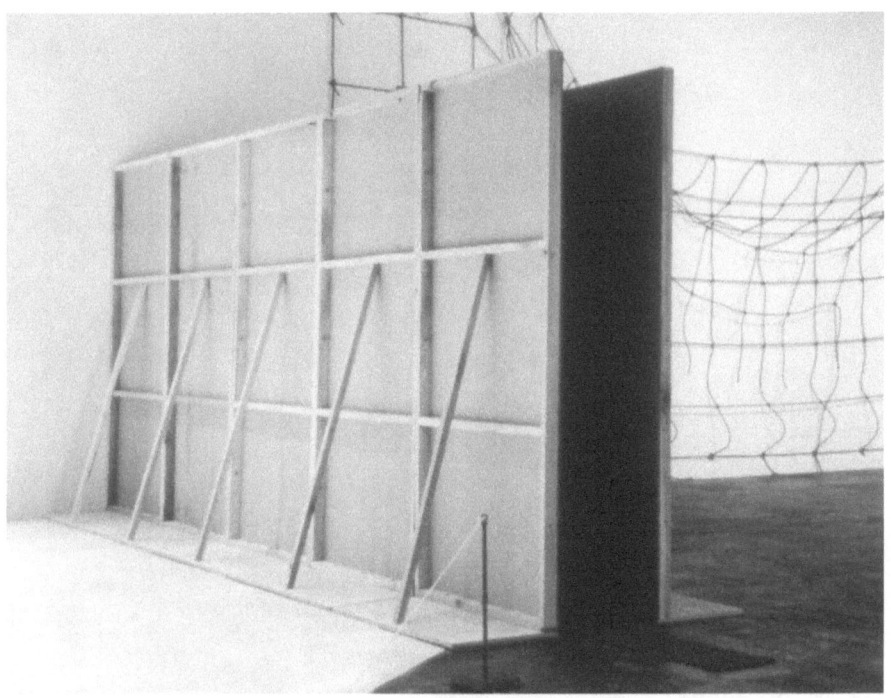

Bruce Nauman, *Performance Corridor*, 1969. Installation view from "Anti-Illusion" exhibition at the Whitney Museum, New York, 1969. *Performance Corridor*, a wooden corridor sculpture that viewers are invited to enter, is flanked by other works from the exhibition. Copyright 2008 Bruce Nauman / Artists Rights Society (ARS), New York.

screens bar viewers from exiting on the opposite side, while their glowing monitors beckon from inside the shadowy enclosure. Viewers, eager to decipher the indistinct black-and-white images emanating from the electronic surfaces, are obliged to step in for a closer look. Both screens depict videotaped images of the interior—that is, both show the space where the spectator stands. Different scenes appear on each of the two surfaces, however: the bottom screen runs footage of the empty corridor while the top monitor offers an unexpected, real-time view of the spectator's body.

The viewer's image is unexpected, not only because it appears in the work at all (as in the earlier *Wipe Cycle*) but because of the distorted fashion in which it appears. Because the camera is positioned at the top of the structure, just inside the corridor entrance, viewers appear to move disconcertingly farther away and get smaller as they approach the screen (reflecting

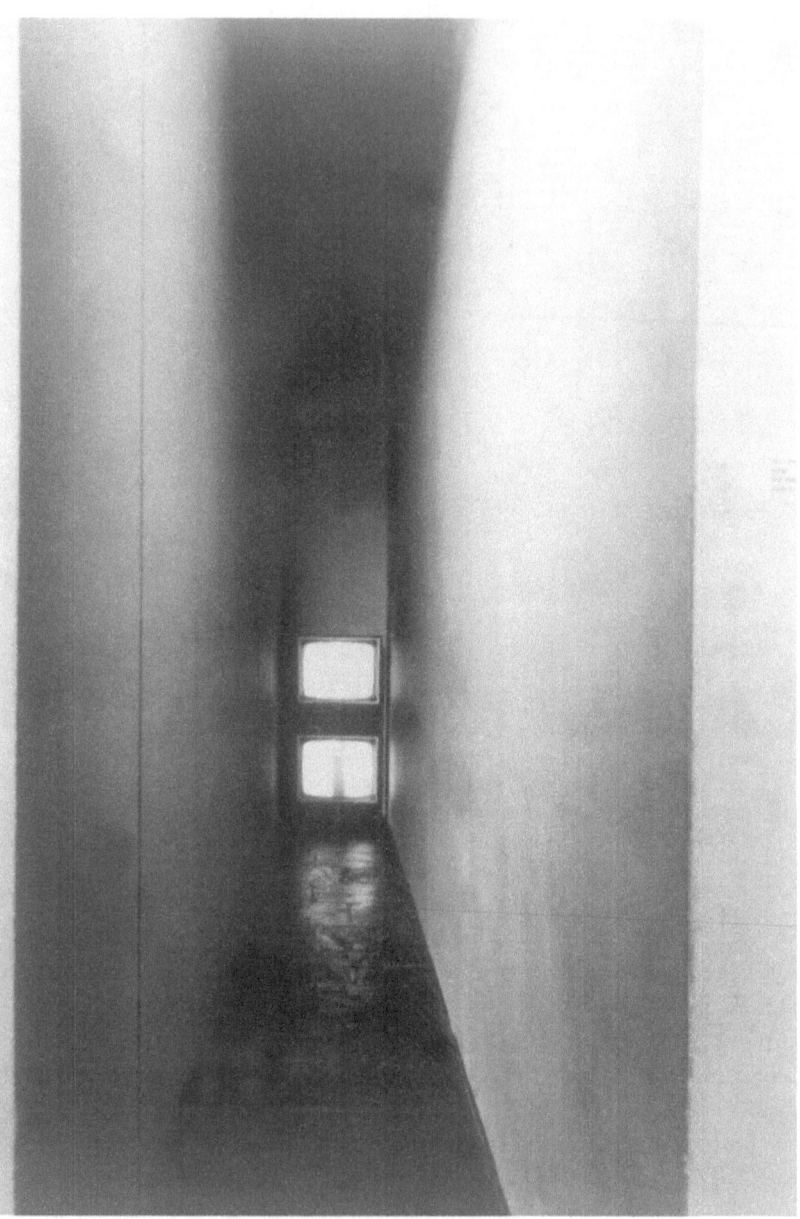

Bruce Nauman, *Live-Taped Video Corridor*, 1970. Wallboard, video camera, two video monitors, videotape player, and videotape. Installation view showing a live closed-circuit video camera mounted just outside the opening of the corridor structure, the footage of which plays back on the upper of the two stacked video monitors. Copyright 2008 Bruce Nauman / Artists Rights Society (ARS), New York.

their actual movement away from the camera). In other words, as viewers move toward the monitors expecting to see a close-up mirror view of themselves at the end of the corridor, they are instead confronted with a disquieting representation of themselves depicted from behind and as moving away from the screen (that is, they see images of their backs retreating from the corridor and away from their own physical bodies). Decidedly uncomfortable with the "critical distance" literally figured on Nauman's media screens, museumgoers are unsettled by the fact that their bodies are never satisfactorily represented on either display. What is rather perverse, of course, is that Nauman's camera and monitor setup ensures that spectators will never achieve the mirrorlike proximity between bodily experience and its representation that they struggle to attain. Participants are obligated to see themselves in an unfamiliar way or, more precisely, to see themselves from the position from which others might see them.

Jacques Lacan's theorization of the gaze captures this psychic effect. Spectators perceive the effects of the gaze because their estranged screen representations allow them to momentarily see themselves as objects.[13] In this sense, closed-circuit video works that incorporate the viewer's image make visible the inaccessible: spectators see themselves through the eyes of another viewer (that is, from the position from which the Other sees the subject). Significantly, this mediated view does not seamlessly match up with the spectator's own perceptual expectations. For Lacan, this is emblematic of the contemporary subject's radically contingent condition: the gaze does not "see" the subject and yet is integrally related to the subject's desire. From a psychoanalytic perspective, this disconnect ultimately produces a split subject. In the case of *Live-Taped Video Corridor*, however, an additional operation is at work, something closer to what the art historian Parveen Adams classifies as the feeling of being "split by the screen."[14]

However perplexing the representations on the top monitor may be for Nauman's audience, *Live-Taped Video Corridor*'s bottom monitor is potentially even more unsettling. Critical theorist Samuel Weber's effort to define the ontology of television borrows in part from Lacan's model of vision and offers another way to decipher the viewer's discomfort when faced with their not-quite-right mediated images. "What we see on the television screen is not so much 'images' but *another kind of vision*, a vision of the other (to be understood as both an objective and subjective genitive).... What we see, above and beyond the content of the images, is someone or something seeing."[15] While the top monitor offers the spectator unexpected (but nonetheless identifiable) real-time self-images, the

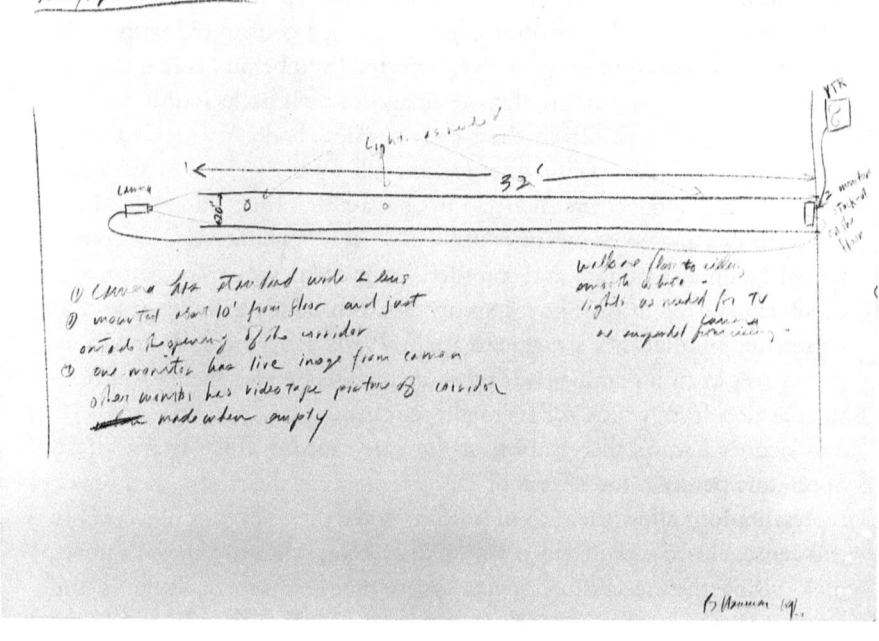

Bruce Nauman, *Live-Taped Video Corridor*, 1970. Artist's
diagram of the work indicating the placement of the camera
and monitors within the gallery space. Copyright 2008 Bruce
Nauman / Artists Rights Society (ARS), New York.

monitor underneath effectively "screens out" the spectator altogether. If,
following Weber, we conceive of video screens as "someone or something
seeing," the bottom monitor's playback is especially disturbing because it
distressingly fails to "see" the spectator at all.

Media scholar Margaret Morse echoes this interpretation and speculates that the viewer's experience with the disobedient twin monitors in
Live-Taped Video Corridor cannily demonstrates the role of media technologies in actively defining contemporary visuality. Schooled to expect
one's own reflection in encounters with video feedback systems, the blank
corridor footage on the lower monitor abruptly unsettles the viewing subject. After all, "there is a human need for and pleasure in being recognized
as a partner in discourse," postulates Morse, "even when the relation is based
on a simulation that is mediated by or exchanged with machines."[16] Not
surprisingly then, contemporary media subjects experience a disarming
sense of loss of self in the face of their screen-based annihilation.

The expectations and conditioned habits associated with viewing video screens in everyday life therefore influence how spectators interact with media technologies in an art context.[17] Beyond the basic requirement that viewers enter and explore the sculpture's oppressively narrow passageway, Nauman purposely structures the viewer's physical and psychic experience with the work by playing on the learned conventions of screen-mediated communication. Among these cultural habits are the generalized tendency of viewers to turn their attention toward video monitors, their desire to see comprehensible screen-mediated representations (or, perhaps more accurately, "confirmations") of themselves, and, finally, the presumption of video's "liveness."[18] Conditioned by network television to understand news coverage as "live," spectators assume that the feedback on both of the artwork's monitors displays real-time images of the corridor and should therefore confirm their presence within the space. The empty corridor imagery that appears on the bottom screen upsets this conventional assumption; like so much presumably live television footage, the shots of this vacant space were prerecorded. The illuminated screens and live moving images in closed-circuit video environments such as Nauman's coax museumgoers to carefully structure their viewing and deftly arrange their bodies in specific ways. In this sense, the viewer's experience with the corridor works is less about built architecture than an architecture of media screen spectatorship—a mutually informing and psychically charged phenomenal connection between the viewing body and the display screen.

Video Corridor for San Francisco (Come Piece) (1969), Nauman's earliest closed-circuit video piece, is an especially instructive example of screen-based manipulation in that, despite its name, the installation does not employ a physical corridor. Instead it is composed of an empty room inhabited by two closed-circuit video cameras and their displays. The cameras are mounted across from each other on opposite walls of the gallery and paired with mismatching monitors on the gallery floor below. That is, each monitor and camera pair is arranged so that the display depicts live images of the space in front of the camera on the opposite side of the room, as opposed to representing the space in front of "their" camera. Upon entering the gallery, viewers traverse from one side of the room to the other to check out the flickering screens in the otherwise deserted space. In so doing they unavoidably walk between the two wall-mounted cameras, subjecting themselves, as in the earlier corridor piece, to the work's cunning, if somewhat playful, surveillance.

Viewers quickly realize that they can see their own images represented on the screens if they carefully adjust their bodies and stand "just so"—

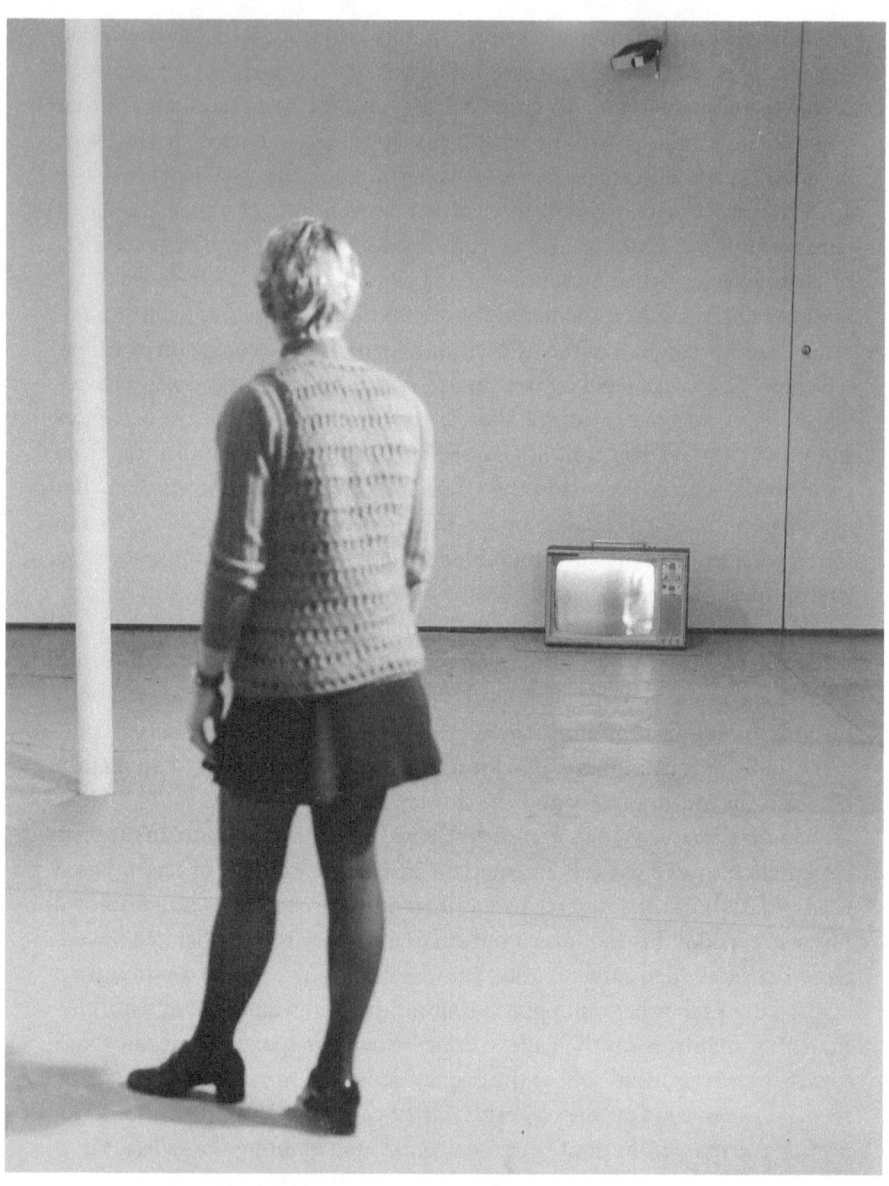

Bruce Nauman, *Video Corridor for San Francisco (Come Piece)*,
1969. The work consists of two video cameras and two monitors.
The installation view shows a spectator observing an inverted
image of herself on one of the two monitors. Copyright 2008
Bruce Nauman / Artists Rights Society (ARS), New York.

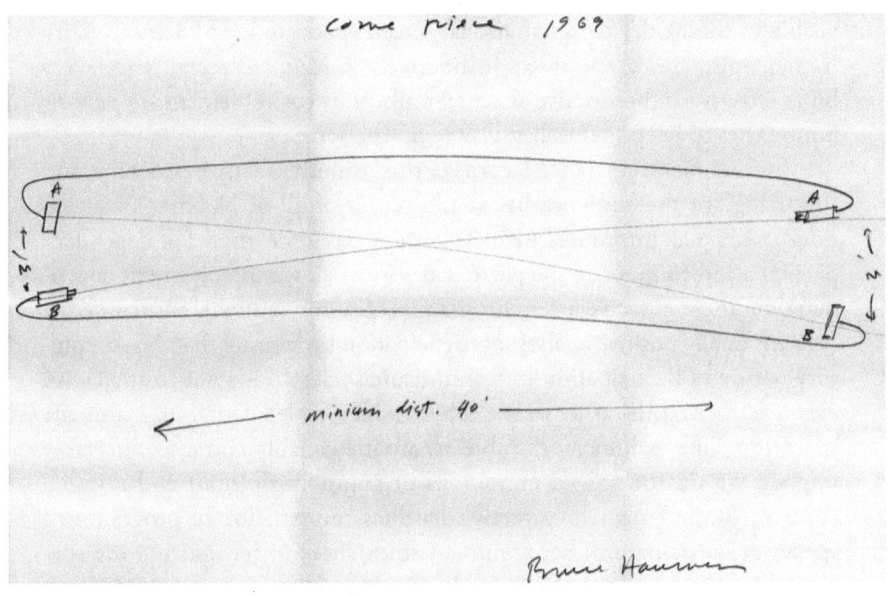

Bruce Nauman, *Video Corridor for San Francisco (Come Piece)*, 1969. Artist's diagram of the work indicating the "mismatched" placement of the two cameras and two monitors at opposite ends of the gallery space. Copyright 2008 Bruce Nauman / Artists Rights Society (ARS), New York.

stationed directly in line with one of the cameras, eyes trained steadily on the monitor opposite. And yet, this is not as easy to achieve as it may sound. The camera does not always point at the monitor and the lenses are turned from time to time, making it extremely trying to line things up satisfactorily. "It's hard to stay in the picture," Nauman admits. "You have to watch the monitor to stay in the picture and at the same time stay in the line of the camera."[19] One's sought-after screen representations are both challenging to achieve and, like *Live-Taped Video Corridor,* profoundly disorienting. Because the screen directly in front of the viewer depicts a view taken by the camera located on the opposite wall (as opposed to depicting a view from the camera directly in front of the viewer as expected), Nauman's spectators again find themselves in the curious situation of seeing themselves getting smaller as they draw closer to the screen's electronic imagery.[20]

The artist's calculated use of the video apparatus severely restricts the precise spatial boundaries in which the spectator's participatory experience may occur; as Nauman puts it, this installation is "like the corridor pieces only without the corridors."[21] In attempting to keep themselves visible in the work's representational screen space, to keep themselves "in frame," so to speak, spectators instinctively fashion a carceral space every bit as effective and restrictive as actual walls. Viewers implement *self-policing* boundaries to keep themselves visible on the screen.

For art historian Janet Kraynak, this "simultaneous beseeching and thwarting" of the audience lies at the center of all of Nauman's installations.[22] Kraynak introduces Alain Touraine's economic model of dependent participation to theorize the particular sort of viewer involvement engendered by these coercive art environments. Touraine's model overturns the conventionally positive analysis of participation by arguing that the compulsory nature of participation in technocratic society leads not to subjective empowerment, but rather to the subject's inevitable alienation. Nauman's spectators, like technocracy's subjects, are inescapably and uncomfortably trapped within the related conditions of compulsory input and external control. While Kraynak correctly identifies the paradox of programmed spectator participation, her argument stops short of recognizing the specifically *screen-based* conditions of the viewer's controlled experience, such as the self-regulation provoked by the video corridors and other closed-circuit video works.[23]

For Adams, in contrast, Nauman's video corridors offer provocative, critical explorations of precisely this issue of self-regulation. Foucault's panopticon model of modern subjectivity famously relies upon the idea of external monitoring (by the guard hidden in the central tower) coupled with the *internalization* of this observation by the subject. Adams argues that Nauman's video corridors shatter the internalization of surveillance by undermining the system of vision it relies on. The video corridors reveal the difference between watching oneself and being watched, which in turn undermines one's perceptual expectations and opens a space to "see differently." Adams's psychoanalytic reading profitably theorizes the psychological impact of the video corridors: the observing subject earns a brief escape, even a sort of liberation, by becoming aware of the incongruous nature of visual surveillance. (Or, to put it in psychoanalytic terms, viewers become aware of the split between the eye and the gaze.) However, this account too leaves the viewer's physical, bodily experience with screen-based technologies unexplored—an issue that is crucially important for closed-circuit installations. Even while aspects of external *visual* control are unveiled in the video corridors, it is equally significant that viewers themselves routinely and voluntarily constrain their physical placement in relationship to the cameras and screens.

To the extent that both the screen-based video apparatus and the audience's habits and expectations for the technology literally move viewers in particular ways, the active participation element of these works clearly constitutes a constricted request or demand. In his *Suspensions of Perception,* Crary describes how a sustained critique of various technologies of attention unites Debord and Foucault's otherwise divergent theorizations of contemporary social relations. If for Debord spectacle works to isolate, separate, and immobilize subjects despite their intense intercommunication, and if for Foucault docile subjects respond to internalized disciplinary initiatives, both thinkers nevertheless understand attention to be an influential, noncoercive power mechanism of late capitalism. Building from these dual models to think through the ideological function of television and the personal computer in particular, Crary contends that, in their dominant uses, these technologies produce stationary, passive, and isolated subjects. Screen-based spectatorship is thus understood as a disciplinary process that regulates viewers' minds and bodies in specific ways geared toward docile productivity.[24]

It is the very limits of the preceding criticism, however, that installations such as *Wipe Cycle* and the video corridors put to the test. Crary himself hints at a dialectic in his acknowledgment that capitalism can never fully rationalize the exchange between the body and the screen, a circuit he compellingly identifies as "the site of a latent but potentially volatile disequilibrium."[25] If Crary is right, then it is reasonable to conclude that there is a prospective criticality embedded in critically reflexive artworks that explore the charged relationship between bodies and screens, even while they make use of coercive technologies of attention. In the final section of this chapter we shall see how Graham's pivotal video work *Present Continuous Past(s)* (1974), like the earlier pieces by Gillette, Schneider, and Nauman, purposefully exploits this volatile relationship and assiduously negotiates the unstable equilibrium between participation and regulation intrinsic to media screen-reliant installation spectatorship.

"Moving" Images: Dan Graham's *Present Continuous Past(s)*

Present Continuous Past(s) consists of a white room with mirrored walls on two adjacent sides. A monitor and camera are mounted on the third, mirrorless wall and the partial fourth wall marks the work's entrance. The camera records everything in front of it, both the spectator's image and the entire room reflected in the glass. This information is played back on the monitor, but with an eight-second delay that introduces a series of discontinuous body images spread out in eight-second intervals. Whereas *Wipe Cycle* and the video corridors present viewers with only one unruly representation at a time, Graham's installation superimposes several moving images of its audience. This produces a peculiar, decentering effect for gallerygoers as they move cautiously throughout the space, struggling to come to terms with seeing multiple versions of themselves in "continuous pasts." This arrangement is made increasingly complex by the fact that, as in *Wipe Cycle,* multiple viewers can engage *Present Continuous Past(s)* concurrently. Viewers are asked to consider how their bodies (virtual or otherwise) are placed in relationship to other members of the audience. While self-conscious viewers may long to step back and observe from afar, they are obliged to actively participate in the sense that competing multiple images of their bodies and those of other participants will be visible on the mirrored walls and video screen no matter what they do.[26]

If the mirrored walls return the viewer's real-time image, the images on the video display follow a different logic. Graham has carefully considered the difference between the viewer's perceptual experience with mirrors and screens: "Mirrors reflect instantaneous time without duration," he explains in a 1975 interview with critic RoseLee Goldberg. "They totally divorce our exterior behavior from our inside consciousness, whereas video feedback does just the opposite; it relates the two in a kind of *durational time flow.*"[27] While mirrors can be employed to produce curious *spatial* displacements in their viewers, video screens have the potential to generate novel spatial *and* temporal experiences. Indeed, Graham's spectators find their bodies simultaneously immersed in a morass of screen-reliant temporalities: the recent past (on the monitor), the present (in the mirror), and the idea of a future time (spectators not only see the actions that they recently performed, but also know that what they do subsequently will soon become visible on the screen as what they have just done).

Gilles Deleuze's writings on Bergson and the cinema offer a useful comparison here.[28] In his profoundly influential book *Matter and Memory,* Bergson proposes that it is artificial to separate what happened in the past from the present or the future, since memory effectively combines them in unending, dynamic movement.[29] Although Deleuze invokes the cinema as the ideal metaphor for demonstrating Bergson's thesis that "peaks of present" and "sheets of past" meet only in the brain (or, in the case of Deleuze's cinema example, on the screen), the superimposed time images on the screen in *Present Continuous Past(s)* arguably offer an even tidier example of the amalgamation between past and present, virtual and actual.[30] Immersed

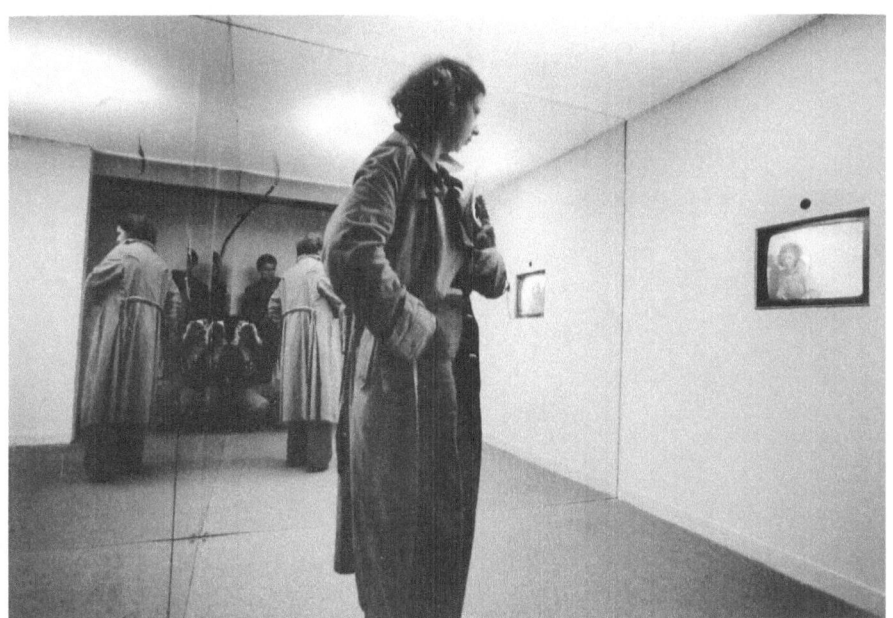

Dan Graham, *Present Continuous Past(s)*, 1974. Mirrored wall,
video camera, and monitor with time delay. This installation
view shows a spectator observing a time-delayed image
of herself on the monitor adjacent to the mirrored walls.
Reproduced from *Video-Architecture-Television: Writings on
Video and Video Works, 1970–1978 / Dan Graham*, edited by
Benjamin H. D. Buchloh (Halifax: Press of the Nova Scotia
College of Art and Design, 1979). Courtesy of Marian Goodman
Gallery, New York.

simultaneously in (at least) three competing temporalities, Graham's viewers
experience time as a constantly shifting process.

Joselit too theorizes the relevance of the destabilizing and shifting spatio-
temporal experience central to early video installations such as Graham's.
For Joselit, this is especially significant due to the way in which these artworks call attention to the subject's relationship to dominant uses of video
technology in everyday life, namely commercial television. In his recent
book, *Feedback: Television against Democracy*, Joselit contends that by breaking open the closed system of television, video practitioners in the 1970s,
such as Graham and Nauman but also Peter Campus, Joan Jonas, and Vito
Acconci, were able to reveal and critique televisual discipline. Graham, he
argues, "brilliantly maps commercial television in reverse by acknowledging
the political atomization and impotence it masks."[31] For the art historian,

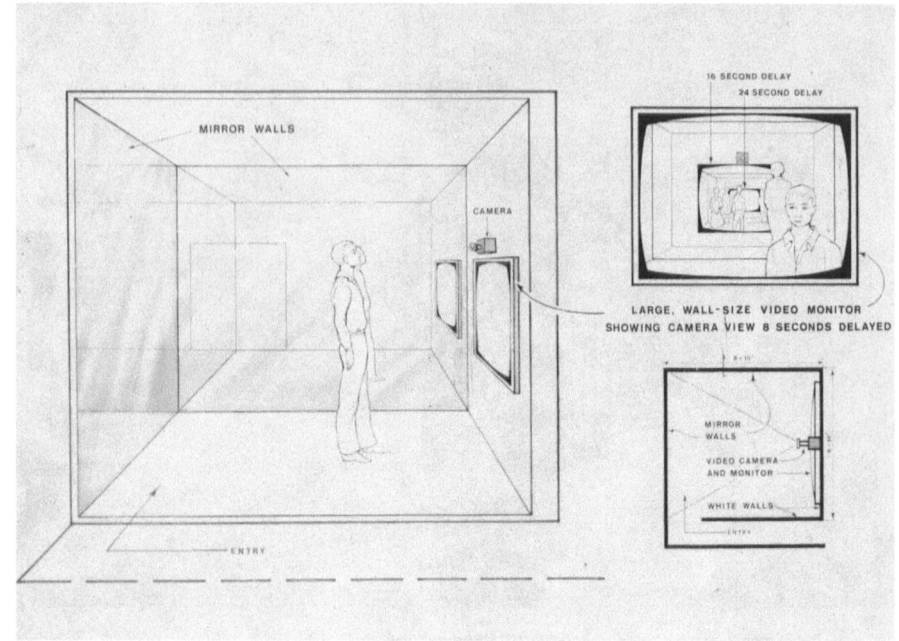

Diagram of Dan Graham's *Present Continuous Past(s)*, 1974.
This diagram indicates the arrangement of mirrors, camera,
and monitor in relationship to the audience and their time-
delayed images. Reproduced from *Video-Architecture-
Television: Writings on Video and Video Works, 1970–1978 /
Dan Graham.* Courtesy of Marian Goodman Gallery, New York.

this is a largely conceptual and psychological operation specifically centered on the viewer's conventional relationship to, and identification with, television's idealized personality types; thus, the critical efficacy of feedback images is how they "represent identity as a *process,* not a televisual *presence.*"[32] Joselit argues that these art objects productively destabilize and multiply identity, bringing into being what philosopher Jacques Rancière refers to as a constructive "in-betweeness."[33]

For the purposes of the present argument, what is most interesting is Joselit's acknowledgment that the criticality of closed-circuit installations exceeds the deconstruction of fixed televisual identity. In revealing the disciplinary conditions of normative television viewing, works such as *Present Continuous Past(s)* also establish "a different sort of relation between a person and his image," one "premised on proximity and touch." He continues:

"It might be tempting to call such an interaction narcissistic [Krauss], but in fact it is the contrary: instead of collapsing the viewer into her picture, the projection appears as an external object, soliciting a response."[34] Although Joselit offers single-channel works by Acconci and Jonas as exemplary of this condition, one might easily extend his argument to encompass key video installation art works as well. *Present Continuous Past(s)*, for example, creates a distance between one's body and screen-based images of that body, which in turn allows viewers a greater reflexivity regarding the relationship of their physical persons to the media screen apparatus. That is, the bewildering video screen representations compel the audience to make comparisons with their actual lived bodies; they must study the behavior of their corporeal selves to understand whether the times and images represented on the video screen are "accurate." Scrutinizing the material and indeed immaterial correlation between one's body and one's screen representation — "Was I smiling in the past?" "Am I smiling now?" — makes it possible to decipher the existence of multiple yet divergent self-images and to figure out Graham's time-delay system. In this way, *Present Continuous Past(s)* tweaks video technology's association with discipline and attention but also, and more specifically, underlines the embodied, material relationship between the viewer and the screen-based apparatus. Like the video works by Gillette and Schneider and by Nauman, the piece obliges its audience to confront the ambiguity of media installation's participatory requirement by drawing out the typically ignored architecture of spectatorship between viewing subjects and media art objects.

Thus, while the disciplinary aspects of screen-reliant spectatorship are undeniable, certain artworks critically contort the condition of audience participation with media environments in creative and disruptive ways. In challenging technologies of attention and control from within, as it were, these installations provocatively underscore the ways in which everyday mass media viewing conventions condition how spectators interact with screen-reliant objects inside the art gallery, even as they insist upon the centrality of the viewers' embodied experience in generating the work's meaning. Chapter 3 extends the analysis of the charged relationship between bodies and screens by assessing the temporal qualities of media installation's reception in more recent artistic production. As we shift our focus to the viewer's temporal experience with screen-based film and video environments created since the mid-1990s, we shall see how the question of just who is disciplining whom becomes ever more complex.

3. **Installing Time** Spatialized Time and Exploratory Duration

The "other cinema" of today . . . emerges as an attempt to insert spatial modes into the temporal dimension, and to "install time" in space. Installing time is a matter of choosing the right spatial model, the most adequate "schematism" allowing the translation of temporal properties into space.

—DANIEL BIRNBAUM, Chronology

It is well known that installations made with time-based media have become increasingly pervasive since the 1990s, aided by the enthusiastic institutional embrace of this now predominant art form and exemplified in celebrated screen-reliant sculptures by artists such as Tacita Dean, Eija-Liisa Ahtila, Douglas Gordon, Doug Aitken, Bruce Nauman, Pierre Huyghe, Pipilotti Rist, Sam Taylor-Wood, and Stan Douglas. The temporal dynamics of post-1990 screen-reliant installation art have been rigorously assessed in recent years by scholars in art history as well as film and media studies.[1] In spite of important differences in their specific arguments, these critics share an interest in the way in which "exhibiting" film and video in art galleries allows viewers a critical standpoint from which to better understand the intricacies of time itself in our media culture. This chapter complicates the current discourse surrounding temporal experimentation in media installation art by drawing attention to an aspect that remains undertheorized: the multiple and sometimes contradictory durational impulses at work in the presentation of moving images to moving bodies in space.

As evocative attempts to, in critic and curator Daniel Birnbaum's words, "install time in space," the many media installations created since 1990 that use time as a material are as variegated as they are abundant. Prominent examples range from a classic Hollywood horror movie extended over approximately twenty-four hours and projected onto a transparent screen (Gordon) to a panoramic, eight-hour quasidocumentary video of an artist's studio screened onto four walls (Nauman), a rapid-fire circular narrative played out on eight screens across three rooms (Aitken), and a richly textured twenty-four-minute film projected onto two adjacent screens (Ahtila). Close readings of these four familiar works—Gordon's *24 Hour Psycho* (1993), Nauman's *Mapping the Studio I (Fat Chance John Cage)* (2001), Aitken's *electric earth* (1999), and Ahtila's *Consolation Service* (1999)—will allow us to investigate the overlapping and at times conflicting temporal impulses—artistic, institutional, individual—that structure the viewer's experience with these screen-reliant pieces.

While the audience's expected time commitment is putatively pre-ordained in the case of viewing non-installation variants of film or video (such as experimental film or single-channel videotapes, whose discrete duration implies some sort of closure, however unresolved), viewers routinely enjoy what one might call an exploratory duration in observing gallery-based media installations: that is, spectators autonomously determine the length of time they spend with the work.[2] Largely unburdened by externally imposed timetables, museum visitors of film and video installations appear to be free to walk in or out at any time. As Fredric Jameson has observed about video in a different context, "We can always shut [it] off, without sitting politely through a social and institutional ritual."[3] This chapter extends chapter 2's analysis of the charged relationship between bodies and media screens by investigating the multifaceted conditions that grant viewers the apparent autonomy to determine how long they will observe moving-image installations, as well as the critical import of the ambulatory observer's shifting power. What might promote the audience's self-directed "window shopping" approach toward these spatialized time-based objects?[4] Could there be something structural to the work itself that incites or compels the spectator's perceived temporal self-sufficiency? If not, who or what is in charge and to what effect? And finally, does the institutional framework of the art gallery oblige viewers to stay to see all of the film or video footage or, in a seeming paradox, might it invite them to keep on strolling at their own pace?

As we shall see in what follows, the individualized, exploratory duration of engaging gallery-based installations is central to the complexity of screen-reliant installation, both in terms of its critical leverage and its ideological function. This open-ended mode of engagement is routinely praised for allowing alternate modes of interaction with media technologies and with the structure of time itself. At the same time, however, this form of spectatorial empowerment is one easily reabsorbed into the fabric of normative culture. Analyzing the differing durational requirements in the widely recognized installations by Douglas, Nauman, Aitken, and Ahtila serves to complicate extant theories of media installation temporality, which have largely overlooked the issue of the viewer's shifting power vis-à-vis private control over durational engagements with screen-based media technologies.

"That's the Only Now I Get"

It is important to recognize that recent experimentation with spatializing time and duration, as well as its critical reception, has an important precedent in media installation art of the 1960s and 1970s.[5] From the time-delay video and mirror installations of artists like Joan Jonas and Dan Graham to the film environments of Michael Snow and Anthony McCall, many artists working with media technologies in the 1960s and 1970s aspired to explore and disrupt the perceived temporal mandates of the era. Art historian Christine Ross explains that early video art (and video installation in particular) is best understood as a series of experiments with modes of *making* time; the medium of video functioned within the visual arts as a privileged means by which to "disrupt dominant conventionalities of time, notably acceleration and temporal linearity."[6] Self-conscious experimentation with the exhibition of time and the viewer's relationship to it was also especially apparent in the work of certain structuralist filmmakers. Largely working within the visual arts, many of these media artists deconstructed the cinema's material and ideological apparatus, which included challenging both the primacy of the image and the temporality of cinematic reception. As early as 1966, filmmaker and theorist Malcolm Le Grice perceived a widespread interest in working with duration as a part of the " 'concrete' dimension of cinema and cinema experience."[7] Writing in 1978, film artist Paul Sharits offered a sort of manifesto for film installations (what he calls "locational" works): Film, according to Sharits, can overcome the passive spectatorship conditions of cinema and "manifest democratic ideals" if, and only if, "the form of presentation does not prescribe a definite duration of respondent's observation (i.e., the respondent may enter and leave at any time)."[8]

Sharits is exemplary of the many artists working in the 1960s and 1970s who identified a progressive, disruptive potential in creating participatory film and video environments that invited spectators to reflect upon dominant modes of experiencing time-based media. On the one hand, allowing viewers to determine the length of time they spent with a film or video was related to a general impulse toward spectator participation in the 1960s and 1970s—promoting the reader over the author, among other reversals. This mode of engagement functioned even more specifically, however, as a calculated critique of conventional media forms and mainstream media viewing experiences (a project inspired in large part by the era's decisive shift toward examining the representational codes of cinema in radical criticism of narrative film and apparatus theory in particular).[9] In terms of the present-day relevance of this model, what is most important to emphasize is the continued focus on open-ended temporality in contemporary screen-reliant installations and their critical reception, in spite of significantly altered artistic, institutional, and ideological conditions.

With this historical context in mind, we can turn our attention to the various temporalities associated with more recent installations, such as Gordon's now infamous *24 Hour Psycho* (1993), that self-consciously trouble the exhibition and reception of media time. Curator and critic Hans-Ulrich Obrist's felicitous term "time readymade" goes a long way toward describing the provocation underlying this work.[10] In Gordon's installation, archival film footage of Alfred Hitchcock's classic thriller *Psycho* (1960) is projected silently at dramatically reduced speed. Snubbing film's normal projection rate of twenty-four frames a second, Gordon extends the original recording to a Warholesque running time of approximately twenty-four hours. The sluggish narrative is visible from both sides of a modestly sized translucent screen that sits at the far end of an otherwise vacant gallery space. *Psycho* is nearly instantly recognizable by visitors, whether or not they have seen the original film. The extreme slowness of the eerily soundless footage permits the audience to make out new details and connections in the now slightly estranged original. Indeed, the narrative flow of Gordon's found temporal object is stymied until viewers painstakingly stitch a particular scene together almost frame by frame.

The question of how long visitors will stick around to view this protracted projection achieves a new urgency here. As specified in the title, it is promptly apparent that viewers will not be able to view the whole film. Institutional screening time and viewing time are suddenly unhinged. With a running time of a full day or more (would it require forty-eight hours to see everything from *both* sides of the screen?), it is impractical for any

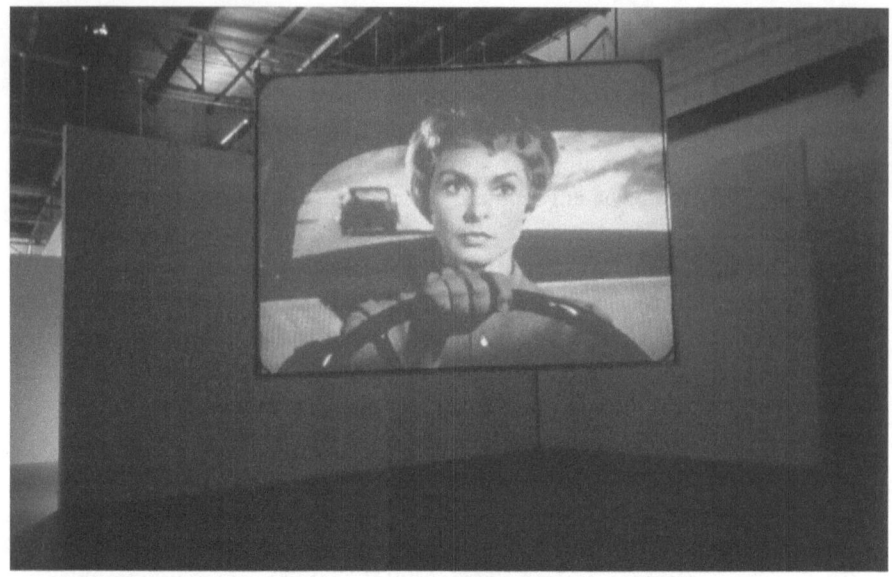

Douglas Gordon, *24 Hour Psycho,* 1993. Installation view from
exhibition at Museum of Contemporary Art, Los Angeles, 2001.
Hitchcock's classic film (the playing time of which has been
extended to approximately twenty-four hours) is projected on
a large screen suspended in the middle of the gallery space.
Courtesy of Douglas Gordon and Gagosian Gallery. *Psycho,*
1960, dir. Alfred Hitchcock, Universal Studios; copyright
Universal Studios.

visitor to see the entire film. "Realistically, no one can watch the whole of
24 Hour Psycho," confirms curator Russell Ferguson. "While we can experience narrative elements in it (largely through familiarity with the original),
the crushing slowness of their unfolding constantly undercuts our expectations, even as it ratchets up the idea of suspense to a level approaching
absurdity."[11] The anticipation inherent in the delayed unfolding of Hitchcock's film situates visitors in the present (what is going on now?) and the
future (what is about to happen?) simultaneously. Moreover, the work's slowness weighs so heavily on its viewers that many of them are soon preoccupied with planning their escape.

Gordon shared his thoughts about *24 Hour Psycho*'s ideal spectator
with his brother, David, who recalls the conversation thusly: "He [Douglas
Gordon] went on to imagine that this 'someone' might suddenly remem-
ber what they had seen earlier that day, later that night; perhaps at around
10 o'clock, ordering drinks in a crowded bar with friends, or somewhere

else in the city, perhaps very late at night, just as the 'someone' is undress-
ing to go to bed, they may turn their head to the pillow and start to think
about what they had seen that day. He said he thought it would be interesting for that 'someone' to imagine what was happening in the gallery right
then, at that moment in time when they have no access to the work."[12] In
the artist's mind, the precise duration of one's experience in the here and
now of the gallery space is subservient to the eventual remembering of the
work in another time and place[13]—as if, well after all of the visitors have
left and the doors are securely locked, the gallery remains strangely animated by illuminated images. Somewhere out there, maybe even now,
Janet Leigh is ruthlessly attacked in the shower—but this fanciful recol-
lection unfolds in super slow motion, like a plodding nightmare. The duration of the actual film footage is thus related to the duration of the ideal
viewer's experience generically, but not specifically. One doesn't have to
see Gordon's film all the way through in the museum to be mnemonically
engaged with it later, for maybe even more than twenty-four hours. Spectators are invited to engage Gordon's work on their own timelines and for
the duration of their choosing.

If twenty-four hours seems an utterly impractical viewing time, one
guaranteed to disrupt cinematic patterns of watching a film or video all
the way through, Nauman's seven-channel digital video work *Mapping the
Studio I (Fat Chance John Cage)* (2001) (hereafter referred to as *Mapping
the Studio*) arguably eliminates the prospect of a "complete" viewing altogether.[14] According to critic Peter Schjeldahl, it would take roughly forty
hours and fifteen minutes to miss nothing in any of *Mapping the Studio*'s
seven projections.[15] The piece is composed of four nearly wall-sized and
semitransparent screens positioned next to one another on the floor so as
to make a large, roomlike enclosure.[16] Seven large digital projectors simultaneously emit enormous (twelve feet high by fifteen feet across) gray-green
projections spaced at regular intervals across the four walls/screens.

Spectators enter *Mapping the Studio* from an opening where two of
the four partitions meet. Once inside the dimly lit space, viewers find that
Nauman's work, true to its title, "maps" the environmental goings-on in
the artist's New Mexico workplace.[17] The seven projections that surround
the viewer each represent a different section of Nauman's studio that the
artist—working with hour-long videotapes and only one infrared camera—
painstakingly recorded over forty-two nights in a four-month period.[18] Fleeting, ambient nighttime noises (trains, coyotes, wind, rain, and so on) inter-
mittently enliven the imagery, allowing spectators an almost panoramic view

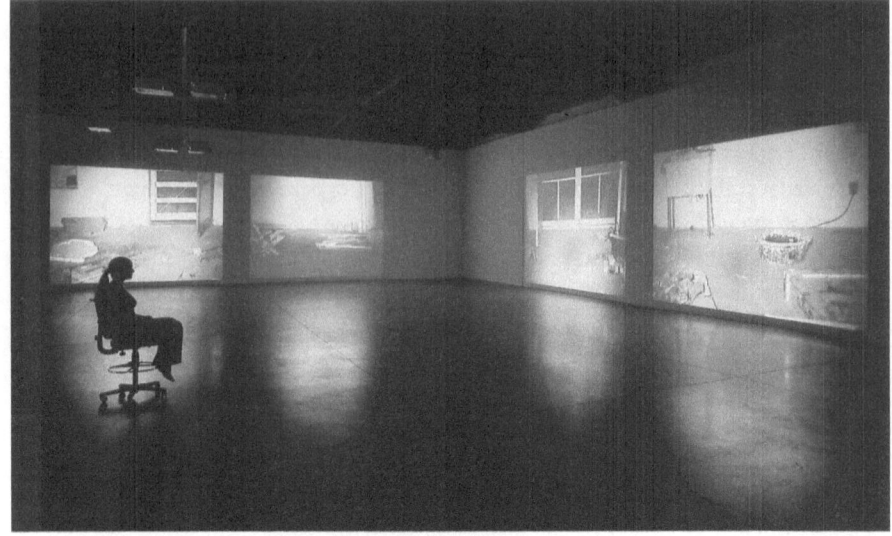

Bruce Nauman, *Mapping the Studio I (Fat Chance John Cage)*,
2001. Installation view of a spectator observing Nauman's
seven-channel, seven-screen video environment as installed
at DIA:Chelsea. (Note that the permanent installation of the
piece at DIA:Beacon described in the text has a slightly
different configuration and does not have seating.) Courtesy
of Sperone Westwater, New York City. Copyright 2008 Bruce
Nauman / Artists Rights Society (ARS), New York.

of the nocturnal sights and sounds in Nauman's work site. (Each of the
seven projectors in the installation is carefully arranged to reconstruct the
original camera position as recorded in the artist's studio, but the images
are spaced at even intervals and not directly adjacent to one another as
they would be in a true panorama.)

As in Gordon's absurdly lethargic movie, very little action is visible on
Mapping the Studio's various wall screens, regardless of the position from
which viewers observe the moving images and regardless of the point in the
narrative at which they happen to encounter the work. Because the documentary images were shot at night in a relatively quiet and empty room,
the artist's cat and a handful of field-cum-studio mice are the sole actors
who periodically interrupt the static silence of what is otherwise a rather
uneventful record of Nauman's mute past creations and works in progress.[19]
"It ends pretty much how it starts. It begins with a title and a few credits,
and then basically it just starts, and then it ends. The image goes blank.
No crescendo, no fade, no 'The End.' It just stops, like a long slice of time,

just time in the studio."[20] While the nearly six-hour video has a linear trajectory, it is carefully structured to downplay those bookends. While the images move, they do not appear to do so with storytelling intent.

Given that *Mapping the Studio* is made up of seven simultaneously projected videos that are each five hours and forty-five minutes long, the artwork's duration could convincingly be described as approximately six hours. The duration of the *spectator's* experience, though, appears to be variable and is instead based on his or her independent actions. Nauman echoes Gordon's desire to fashion an "ongoing object"—a media work that is present even in its very absence: "It just felt like it needed to be so long that you wouldn't necessarily sit down and watch the whole thing but could come and go. . . . I wanted that feeling that the piece was just there, almost like an object, just there, ongoing, being itself."[21] In this description, Nauman notes the *anticipated* duration of the spectator's experience with the installation ("it needed to be so long that you wouldn't necessarily sit down and watch the whole thing but could come and go"), the duration of the videotape itself, and finally the audience's (potentially divergent) *idea* of the work's duration ("I wanted that feeling [for the viewer] that the piece was just there . . . ongoing being itself"). While the footage will eventually conclude, Nauman predicts that viewers will understand the video-based work as something closer to sculpture, something that could be described as perpetually taking place.

In practice, the extremely long (effectively unwatchable) duration of Nauman's *Mapping the Studio*—with its almost infinite possible points of entry and exit and views from which the six hours of multiscreen projections could be watched—highlights the necessarily and even *obligatory* exploratory duration of the viewer's encounter. As with *24 Hour Psycho,* both the extraordinarily long duration of the footage and the fact that the multiple-screen projections have no obvious beginning or ending point to guide the length of one's visit encourage visitors to realize that their experiences will be inevitably partial and incomplete. At the same time, these pieces appear to invite the observer to enter the artwork at any point in the cycle of projections and to explore the environment for the length of time each individual spectator deems appropriate. A viewer may elect to stay inside these installations for six seconds, six minutes, or even six hours, but what is most crucial is that the choice typically is understood to be one that the *spectator,* not the artist, artwork, or institution, will make.

Much like *Mapping the Studio*'s room fabricated from projection screens, the various projection surfaces that comprise Aitken's *electric earth* (1999) merge with the exhibition space's architecture, engulfing several rooms in the case of the latter. *electric earth* presents a fictional narrative about the nocturnal journey of a young black man (dancer Giggy Johnson) moving through an uncannily deserted Los Angeles landscape punctuated by bursting 99-cent stores and barren parking lots. The piece is made up of eight short loops projected onto an equivalent number of opposing screens that spill across three or four conjoined rooms. (Most installations of the work employ three rooms, bifurcating the center room.) The activity of the twitching protagonist, moving between the screens as his twilight voyage progresses through an increasingly fast-paced environment, binds the divergent times and places together in a jerking, stuttered cycle. The inanimate things around Johnson gradually get faster and take on a frantic pace of their own: a Coke machine refuses a dollar bill offering, shopping carts rule a deserted big box parking lot, an electric car window spastically rises and falls of its own accord, and so on. A pulsating sound track of electronic music and industrial sounds seemingly reinforces the frenzied dancing of the protagonist and the curiously animate mediascape that envelops him. The lone character narrates his sudden move from dreamy lounging on a hotel bed, armed with a remote, to energetic meanderings throughout the nondescript urban sprawl: "A lot of times I dance so fast that I become what's around me. It's like food for me. I, like, absorb that energy, the information. It's like I eat it. That's the only now I get."[22] Information sustains but also consumes him. The screen-based media environment nourishes Aitken's anonymous roving urban wanderer even as it threatens to ingest him.

The video's dialogue—"That's the only now I get"—might well describe the gallerygoer's experience. Indeed, it is almost nonsensical to ask how long this video work lasts. Viewers walk at their own pace through the tunnel of rooms, pushed along by the corridorlike arrangement of the gallery spaces as much as by the ostensible progression in the eight short loops that constitute the quasinarrative (the final screen in the last room shows the actor entering a tunnel, which offers a strong sense of closure). Detached from any specific obligation to view all of the imagery and instead compelled to walk amid a barrage of looped images from one side of the media passageway to the other, viewers are rather unsettlingly remade into the protagonist himself, an experience dramatically opposed to the almost meditative stillness embedded in the first two works.

Aitken's stated goal is to employ film and video to contest the linearity seemingly intrinsic to these media technologies. He wants nothing less than to render the question of the media work's duration irrelevant. "Film

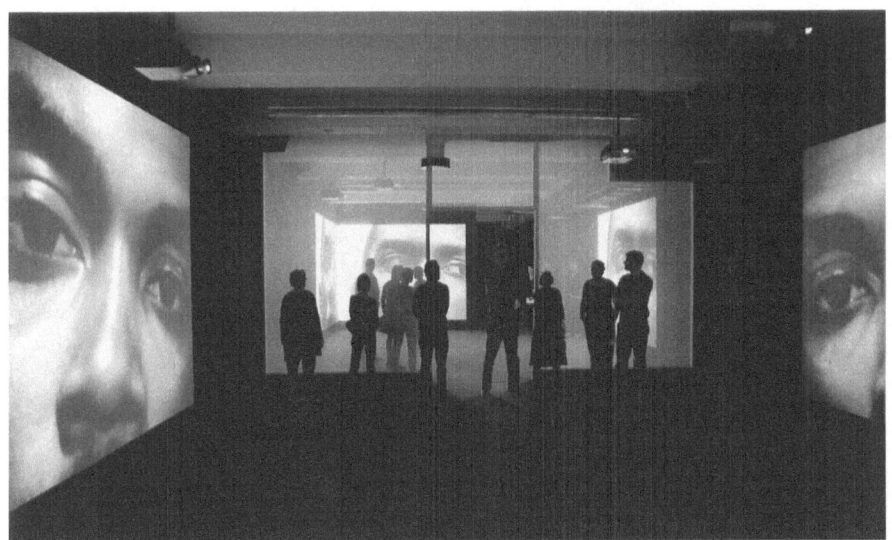

Doug Aitken, *electric earth*, 1999. Installation view showing
temporarily synced imagery in this environmental artwork
consisting of eight short loops projected on an equivalent
number of opposing screens that spill across three to four
conjoined rooms. Courtesy of 303 Gallery, New York.

and video structure our experience in a linear way simply because they're
moving images on a strip of emulsion or tape. They create a story out of
everything because it's inherent to the medium and to the structure of
montage. But, of course, we experience time in a much more complex
way," observes Aitken. "The question for me is, How can I break through
this idea, which is reinforced constantly? How can I make time somehow
collapse or expand so it no longer unfolds in this one narrow form?"[23]
Inasmuch as *electric earth*'s narrative corridor defeats conventional linear
storytelling, however, it does so by making a pact with the overstimulated
peripatetic spectator, granting him or her the privilege of autonomously
crafting *electric earth*'s narrative in exchange for submission to the multiple
flows of sounds and images.

Consolation Service, Ahtila's two-screen film installation, takes yet
another approach to the display of time-based material. The work is an
elaborate fictional narrative screened synchronously on a long, blank wall
at the back of a darkened rectangular gallery space. The two adjacent projections offer different perspectives of the same story, facilitating comparisons between two points of view that overlap only rarely. Whereas other

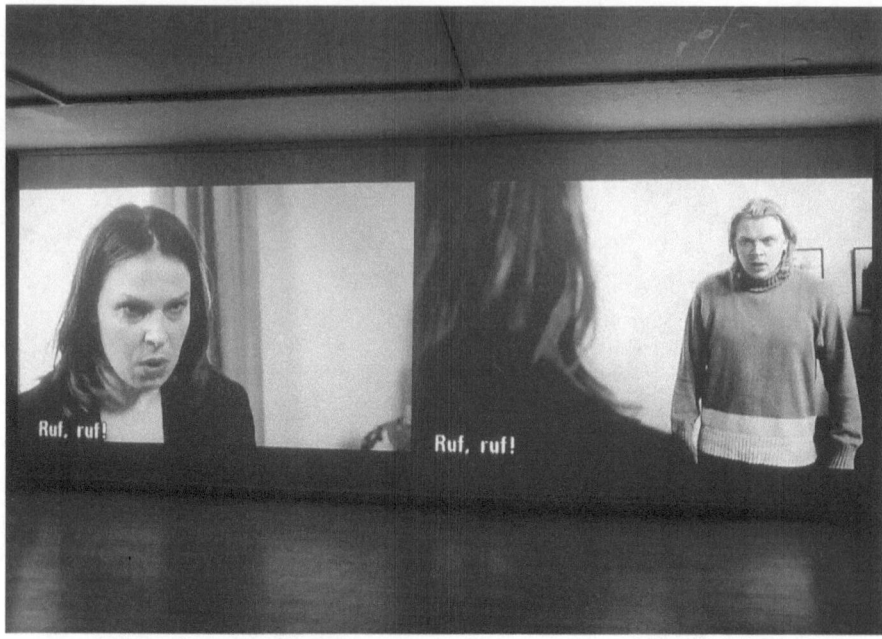

Eija-Liisa Ahtila, *Consolation Service*, 1999. DVD installation,
35 mm film, 23 minutes 40 seconds, 1:1.85, Dolby Surround.
This installation view of the dual-screen film shows two different images from the protagonists' therapy session accompanied by identical subtitles. Courtesy of Marian Goodman
Gallery, New York and Paris. Copyright Crystal Eye Ltd.,
Helsinki.

artists have used this dual screen technique primarily to emphasize spatial
differences (Gordon and Shirin Neshat come to mind), Ahtila's double
screens frequently deconstruct temporal as well as spatial continuity. The
artist explains that one screen is primarily concerned with detail and context shots and the other with moving the narrative along, although this is
not readily apparent on a first viewing.

   Consolation Service presents an intricately layered story about a disen-
chanted young couple—new parents Anni and JP—that recently decided
to divorce. "It's a story about an ending," the narrator confides. Pivotal
events include a therapist guiding the couple through a separation ritual, a
birthday celebration for JP, and the accidental drowning of the couple
and their friends after having fallen through the treacherously thin ice of a
frozen lake. *Consolation Service* weaves countless loops of pastness across

and between the two projections; it is never clear what is fantastical or metaphorical and what, if anything, is "real." For example, Anni reappears unharmed in her empty apartment just after her descent into impossibly cold waters, whereas JP apparently perished in the accident, given that he returns postdrowning as a pixilated apparition longing to achieve peace with his estranged spouse.

Unlike the artworks discussed thus far, Ahtila's film features a lengthy and complex dialogue. A female neighbor recounts the tragic yet mundane (or, better, tragic *because* mundane) story of the ex-lovers in Finnish. English subtitles run across both screens so that a single narration of events accompanies what at times seem to be two opposed story lines. This is just one of the myriad ways in which Ahtila insistently casts viewers out of what might otherwise become a cozy cinematographic cocoon; other examples include having characters sporadically reveal their position as actors and speak directly to the camera, and allowing the actors' dialogue to draw the (never pictured) narrator into the story.

In contrast to the open-ended, spectator-determined duration of Gordon's, Nauman's, and Aitken's installations, there is a sense that you will miss something central to *Consolation Service* if you walk away before the twenty-three-minute, forty-second loop is done. To consequently describe this work as a narrative film is both correct and grossly misleading, however; the events are not linear in any traditional sense and, as stated, the work rewards viewing initiated at any point in the cycle. Although the work does not *need* to be experienced in a linear, start-to-finish fashion—the rich narrative is equally compelling no matter at which point one begins watching it—this piece encourages the audience to observe the imagery in its totality. Comfortable seating and clearly posted running times are among the most apparent cues. The neighbor's impassive yet enchanting narration also contributes to the sense that there is an entire story to know, even if the "story" is multilayered, open-ended, and circular (effectively a loop within a loop). While the fragmentary events are deliberately incapable of presenting an overarching and coherent account, to witness less than twenty-four minutes of *Consolation Service* is, in some sense, to fail to see the work at all. Moreover, that many of Ahtila's installations (including this one) are also conceived as single-screen 35 mm experimental films supports the notion that viewers should preferably see the entire recording.[24] The artist in fact insists that the work be presented to the audience "from start to finish, *as a film.*"[25]

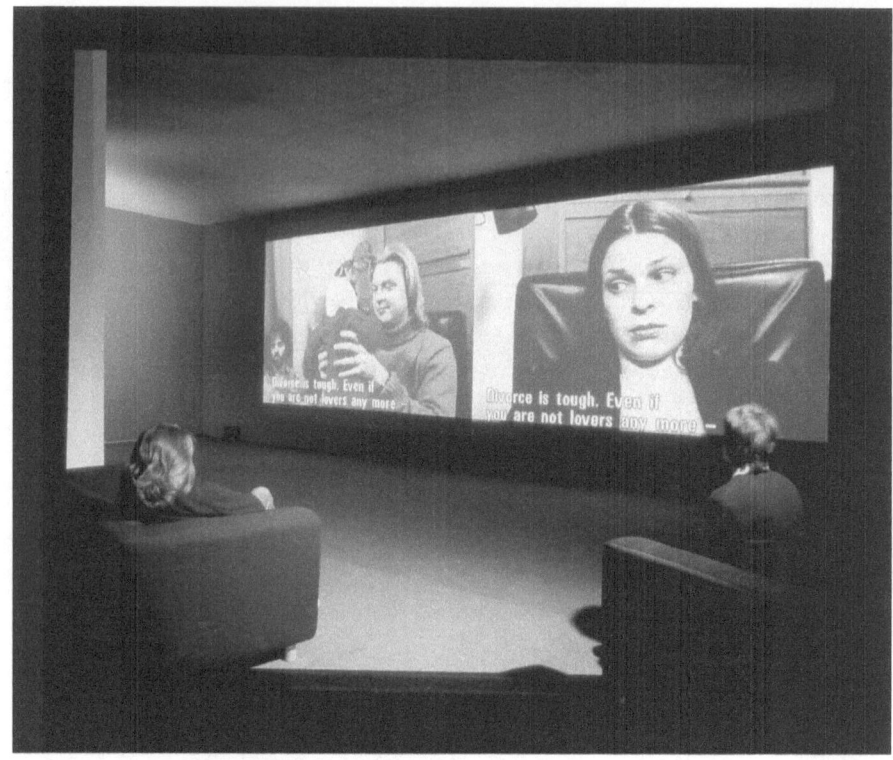

Eija-Liisa Ahtila, *Consolation Service*, 1999. Installation view.
The work was installed in the museum with seating, supporting
the artist's request that the artwork be screened "as a film."
Courtesy of Marian Goodman Gallery, New York and Paris.
Copyright Crystal Eye Ltd., Helsinki.

Lost in, but in Control of, Time

Among the critics who have explored the question of the viewer's experience with these time-based art objects, Jean-Christophe Royoux, for one,
identifies a potentially critical, even "emancipatory" spectatorship in media
art environments by Gordon, Ahtila, Dean, Huyghe, and others. For the
critic, these installations purportedly both deconstruct and exceed dominant
forms of chronology. The "cinema of exhibition," expounds Royoux in a
catalog essay for *Cinéma Cinéma,* is best described as "a loop without a beginning or end, a structure in which the experience of temporality can no
longer be separated from a subjective reconstruction of duration," thereby
"demonstrating the possibility of an alternative to the kind of relationship
to time inherent in cinematographic sequentiality."[26] This critical opera-

tion hinges less on the viewer's experience with moving images than it does on what he calls the phenomenon of immobile or suspended duration: film and video installations generate intensely subjective experiences of time because the viewer is obliged to create mental images and assist in generating the work's narrative. In his framework, the images in *24 Hour Psycho* or *Mapping the Studio,* for example, are powerful for their very *immobility* , since this deferral ideally encourages spectators to mentally complete the piece. This mode of display, concludes Royoux, allows audiences access to another space-time that can "disrupt the homogeneity, regularity and unremitting succession of our own."[27] Philosophy scholar Peter Osborne makes a similar argument in a 2004 essay in which he considers gallery-based film and video in Bergsonian terms: "The marked spatiality of the modes of display of film and video in art spaces . . . and crucially, the movement of the viewer through gallery space, undercuts the false absolutization of time to which cinema is prone." For Osborne, like Royoux, this is fundamentally important because it "highlights the *constructed*—rather than received—character of temporal continuity."[28]

In his recent book *Chronology,* Birnbaum offers another philosophically informed theorization of the potential criticality of the ways in which time is spatialized and put on display in contemporary screen-reliant installations. Indeed, he assigns these artworks a paradigmatic status: "If cinema could produce what Deleuze called crystal-images capturing for an instant the inner workings of time itself, then the temporal possibilities of this 'other cinema', exploring more intricate forms of parallelism and synchronicity, are even greater."[29]

Like Aitken and Royoux, Birnbaum detects a thoroughgoing critique of linearity. This is important because, by challenging the spectator's conventional notion of linearity, these artworks inspire an awareness that the construction of subjectivity is itself an open-ended, durational process. As Husserlian phenomenology makes clear, the layered structure of subjectivity allows for many flows of awareness;[30] in this regard, reminds Birnbaum, the temporal polyphony (Stan Douglas) of multiscreen installations is in fact the mental state in which we all live.[31] The overlapping flows of moving imagery in works such as *electric earth,* for example, allow viewers to recognize the extent to which they *always* live in many different times simultaneously. In *Consolation Service* too time can "crystallize" (Deleuze) in scores of ways but will never coalesce into a coherent, stable conception of the subject. Birnbaum's ultimate contention, then, is that the viewer's phenomenological experience with elaborate assemblages of time-based imagery could productively reveal something about the nature of time itself (although he is quick to clarify that time-consciousness can appear only *indirectly*, through various forms of spatialization).

Film theorist Dominique Païni takes a slightly different approach and pinpoints a dialectic at work in the presentation of moving images to moving bodies. He proposes that "[the] installation of a projection of moving images always institutes a tension . . . in a continuum of images which tends [in the cinema] to be one with the flow of consciousness." In the case of film and video installations, the usual coincidence between the viewer's flow of consciousness and the flow of images in a cinematic, theatrical setting "is countered," according to Païni, by the "random wandering of the flâneur, the visitor/spectator."[32] In other words, one's self-directed perambulations through a given installation make one conscious of film or video's temporal flow because, in this context, the moving imagery is not necessarily in lockstep with the temporal flow of one's own consciousness. While he concedes that it is "impossible by definition to escape this fusion of the two times"—that is, out-of-frame time will unavoidably cross-pollinate with in-frame time, just as perception and memory are always coextensive—Païni concludes that the mobile viewer nevertheless does temporarily disrupt it.[33] What is remarkable for Païni about the exhibition of time in media installations—and here his critique resonates with Birnbaum's—is the way these works can provocatively display the flow of consciousness as it is manipulated, swept up in, and captured by the flow of images. In this scheme, the temporal river that is Giggy Johnson's electric jig through *electric earth*, *Psycho*'s pokey playback, or the flickering surveillance images of Nauman's shadowy studio is temporarily bracketed out, suspended in parentheses alongside the current of the viewer's consciousness.

In contrast to the other critics' implicit optimism regarding media installation's ability to deconstruct habitual temporal relationships to dominant mass media forms, however, Païni remains deeply skeptical about the critical potential of such works and of the move from the cinema to the gallery in general.[34] The specific relevance of viewer mobility and the shifting power dynamic this activates vis-à-vis the media object is central to Païni's larger critique.[35] Discussing the work of what he calls fourth-generation video artists such as Aitken, Rist, and Taylor-Wood, he observes how nomadic viewers negotiate their own trajectory with works such as *electric earth*, creating meaning as they amble along. Païni is cognizant of the flip side of the cinema spectator's alleged "dechaining" or liberation in the gallery: "This renewed physical freedom is no doubt only an illusion, since in one way it is very much of the correlative of the emphasis on the individual as consumer of advertising and art."[36] Installation visitors, declares Païni, are in effect twenty-first-century flâneurs: "Here, quite unexpectedly at this century's end, we witness the return of Baudelaire's flâneur and his experience of seeing time exhibited in the Tuileries by that toy known as the phenakistiscope." These "fin-de-siècle installations" are "bringing back the window-display effect that was given architectural and scenographic form by the Parisian arcades of the nineteenth century," and creating a "paradoxical hybrid of salon- and movie-goer" in the process.[37]

Païni's incisive assessment underlines a fundamentally important aspect of screen-reliant installation spectatorship, although perhaps one not accurately described as flânerie. As film theorist Raymond Bellour points out, today's art galleries furnished with multiscreen moving-image environments are not the outdoor shop windows of the nineteenth-century Parisian arcades.[38] However much contemporary media art viewers may indeed be "just browsing," the fractured, split mass media subject is not Baudelaire's disinterested dandy. Nevertheless, his emphasis on the self-directed mobile spectator is apposite and allows us to think about how certain works, such as *24 Hour Psycho, Mapping the Studio,* and *electric earth,* induce viewers/consumers to choose their own timeline. Even while *Consolation Service* (as described earlier) proffers a markedly different proposition, one that asks its audience to commit to a specific temporal engagement, this proposed mode of engagement contrasts sharply, as Bellour has observed, with the viewer's experience of this piece as presented in large exhibitions.[39]

Reviewing the film and video installations at the notoriously media-centric 1999 Venice Biennale (where both Aitken's *electric earth* and Ahtila's *Consolation Service* made their debuts), art critic and historian Michael Archer offers this sobering observation: "What this mode of presentation has built into it is the inevitability that the work will not be witnessed for very long. All that seems to happen is that you wait a couple of minutes until your feet start to ache from standing still, and then push off again."[40] While the experience of viewing time-based media in large-scale international exhibitions diverges in many ways from appreciating the same pieces in a museum or gallery, both settings tend to support spectator-determined time frames. Pieces such as *Consolation Service* are noteworthy for the way in which they may provocatively disrupt the museum audience's entrenched allegiance to independent roaming,[41] but the alleged disconnect between a given media installation and the museological or institutional durational conventions for this art form warrant further exploration.

Even for viewers habituated to the demands of time-based arts since minimalism (performance, body art, process art, etc.), there is something slightly incongruous about viewing film and video artworks in a museum. This friction is perhaps most palpable in the case of *non*-installation variants of film or video. Different expectations regarding the viewer's temporal commitment to a given genre of media art may even account for video installation's dramatic institutional popularity compared to single-channel video works (individual videotapes)—this according to artist Doug Hall and critic Sally Jo Fifer in the introduction to their influential anthology on video art.[42] The editors go so far as to diagnose a conflict seemingly *inherent* in the reception of noninstallation forms of video, classifying single-channel video as a medium that stages "a viewing experience that is in conflict with the temporality of the museum."[43] Curator Chrissie Iles offers a potential explanation that echoes the sentiments of Hall and Fifer: "Filmmakers in an avant-garde situation insist that you come, quite rightly, and sit in the space and watch their films from beginning to end." Such an arrangement, she concludes, is essentially "*antithetical* to the art world."[44] Sculptural forms of film and video appear to have rendered these screen-based art forms more institutionally palatable, and certainly more institutionally and privately collectable, in part because of their unfixed duration. Film and video deployed in sculptural and architectural configurations accommodate the art-viewing habits of self-directing nomadic visitors who take umbrage with inflexible viewing times.

Given these conditions, it seems reasonable to ask: do viewers prefer installation variants of film and video art because, to paraphrase Jameson, one can always walk off, "without sitting through a polite social and institutional ritual"? Did the disruption of linearity and the critical potential of demystifying the media apparatus in the 1960s and 1970s find its logical counterpart in the disinterested experience-seeking contemporary museum audience? These questions are not entirely new in art historical discourse, but they represent questions underexplored in connection to time-based moving-image environments.[45]

Rosalind Krauss's seminal essay "The Cultural Logic of the Late Capitalist Museum" (1990) offers a partial account.[46] Krauss theorizes how minimalism's originally critical phenomenological project already contained the potential to shift toward what she considers to be the contemporary condition of "degraded" participation that characterizes the subject's experience within the late capitalist museum.[47] In this model, the contemporary museum emerges as a place to experience "experience" and installation spectatorship itself appears to be closely allied with the capitalist tendency to reify individual experience and freedom.

Krauss's model tempers more celebratory accounts of how the viewer's interaction with time-based installations disrupts one's conventional understanding of (media) time. Rigorously investigating the role of the artwork, the individual, *and* the institution in generating particular spectatorship conditions brings the following issues to light: by creating media installations that support or even require visitors to determine the length of their experience with the work, might artists unintentionally provide for a spectatorship characterized by short attention spans? Do they reward itinerant viewers by allowing them to understand the work regardless of when they enter or how long they stay? Spectators generally assume that they are in control of the duration of their experiences with media installations, and indeed the open-ended running times of contemporary film and video environments tend to support this conception. In promoting the spectator's peripatetic participation and specifically the exploratory duration thereof, media installations may, in actual practice, run the risk of overprivileging the viewer's role and implying that all meaning resides in the individual spectator.

Considered this way, the temporal "flânerie" associated with installation spectatorship may, ironically, serve to reinforce an extremely conventional viewing subject. Païni comes closest to capturing the issues at stake by linking this mode of viewership to the nineteenth-century flâneur's experience of window-shopping.[48] As useful as this model is, we might profitably update it by noting the affinity to more recent modes of screen-based window (Windows?) shopping. In the case of viewing screen-reliant artworks, ambulatory art viewers unconsciously endeavor to merge museumgoing habits with those of watching film, TV, and countless other screen-based devices, from PCs to PDAs. (Indeed, Païni insinuates as much in his comment that "the contemporary art gallery and the museum have become home to the desire for screenplays … made for someone other than the captive moviegoer."[49])

Thus, although the dominant critical discourse tends to offer an affirmative view of the way that time is put on display in media installations as constituting a productive critique of the viewer's conventional interactions with commercial media, it is equally important to recognize that the audience's sense of autonomous temporal control may in fact be reflective of

mainstream viewing experiences with screen-based mass media technologies, especially since certain technological developments in the 1990s.[50] As
early as 1993, scholar Anne Friedberg comments upon how the time-
shifting effects of our everyday experiences with the multiplex theater, cable
television, and VCR have reinforced the ways in which today's media
viewing is privately and individually controlled. She asserts: "The cinema
spectator (and the armchair analog, the VCR viewer) with fast forward,
fast reverse, many speeds of slow motion, easily switching between channels
and tape, always able to repeat, replay, return is a spectator *lost in* but also
in control of time."[51] Friedberg's prescient observation—clearly it would
not be a stretch to add Web browsing to Friedberg's list of self-directed
time-shifting activities—permits us to recognize how the spectator's everyday temporal experiences with screen-reliant media both in and outside
the home may inform and reflect present-day installation spectatorship. In
a curious turn, the contemporary media consumer's privately controlled
temporal experiences with film and video in everyday life are unintentionally, albeit logically, reflected in the spectatorship conditions of the very art
form whose early definition was founded upon its alleged difference from
the conditions of mass media spectatorship.

P.S.1 curator Klaus Biesenbach hints at this problematic in the catalog
for his 2001 exhibition *Loop,* which featured installations by Gordon and
Nauman, among others. "With seemingly infinite freedom of choice, a
recurring action becomes a stabilizing factor for the people of the First
World," he writes in regard to the seemingly ubiquitous loop approach for
the production and exhibition of contemporary moving-image works. "Time
appears to be tangible and serviceable, a phenomenon capable of being in-
fluenced, lengthened or repeated. This theme is reflected not only in the
fine arts, but also in the world of media: in pop culture, in techno music,
in endlessly repeated video clips, and in advertising."[52] In this way, the
time-shifting mobile spectator appears to be a close relative of the contemporary media subject; both are *lost in* yet determinedly struggling for
the *control of* their experiences with screen-based technologies.

As critics from Birnbaum to Païni have eloquently proposed, contemporary film and video installations, by putting time itself on display,
uncover something about the nature of temporality in general. The question is what, exactly, do they reveal? In which ways does the shifting
power of the mobile media spectator both incorporate and resist the contemporary media consumer's propensity toward "window shopping"? The

next two chapters build on the analysis of the subjective consequences of the exhibition of time in screen-reliant installations by investigating the spatial dynamics of viewing these works of art. Shifting our principal thematic focus from temporal to spatial conditions, we will nonetheless continue to interrogate the continuities and discrepancies between media installation spectatorship and everyday mass media viewing from the mid-1960s to the present. Chapter 4 examines the conceptual and physical spaces particular to viewing screens in early film and video environments in the 1960s and 1970s—the spaces, that is, in which media art spectators first emerged as screen subjects.

4. Be Here (and There) Now
The Spatial Dynamics of Spectatorship

The screen is a component piece of architecture, rendering a wall permeable to ventilation in new ways: a "virtual window" that changes the materiality of built space, adding new apertures that dramatically alter our conception of space and (even more radically) of time.

—ANNE FRIEDBERG, The Virtual Window

As in everyday life, cinematic and electronic screens in gallery-based installations consistently draw our attention, however fleeting, to the light-based imagery presented on their surfaces. Our cultural habit of immediately looking at media screens and our propensity to view them as windows onto other representational or informational spaces—concentrating on the spaces depicted "on" or "inside" the screen—has special consequences for the complex spatial dynamics of screen-reliant installation art spectatorship. This chapter is concerned with the ways in which space was conceived in the environmental media works that flourished in the midst of widespread artistic experimentation with spatial and temporal phenomena in the late 1960s and 1970s and with the novel viewer-screen interfaces that this ambitious experimentation engendered.

Artists in this era were not alone in their devotion to expanding the spatial and temporal possibilities for film and video. Filmmakers' co-ops in London and New York, as well as certain artists working with structural film and experimental video, shared this generalized ambition toward creating process-based, anti-illusionist media production—although, with a few important exceptions, these media works tended to be less interested in the viewer's phenomenological engagement with the exhibition space and the material art objects it contained than in investigating the properties of film or video in an otherwise unimportant space.[1]

The interest in process-based work that developed (accompanied by varying degrees of political urgency) in the 1970s can be largely attributed to the new theoretical attention to the subject, discourse, and textual and ideological analysis, especially under the influence of the writing of Barthes, Lacan, and Althusser. As critics assigned new importance to the process of reading or viewing, *how* one sees became as relevant as *what* one sees. Not surprisingly, many media art theorists and practitioners roundly rejected illusionist representation, arguing that dominant forms of mass media spectatorship were bound up in the ideological consequences of Renaissance spatial codes of perspective and therefore shared its presumably immobile, disembodied, and idealist viewer.[2]

As we have seen in previous chapters, Annette Michelson and Rosalind Krauss were among the first to introduce the phenomenological and anti-illusionist interpretation of postminimalist media art within a North American context.[3] For these critics, media installations (such as those by Michael Snow and Paul Sharits, among others) were especially noteworthy for the way in which they disrupted illusionistic space by calling attention to the "real" space of the projective situation. In the European context, an especially influential (if problematic) political aesthetic developed with the critical discourse surrounding structural-materialist film.[4] Typical was the argument made by influential London-based filmmaker and theorist Peter Gidal that media artists should enable an analytical form of viewing that would emphasize how subjects are constructed in ideology. For Gidal, filmmakers should deconstruct and reveal the filmic and ideological apparatus (including its illusionistic appeals) via a series of material interventions, including disrupting conventional spatial codes. This self-reflexive operation was assumed to inevitably produce active, empowered spectators categorically distinct from the passive viewers associated with illusionist cinema.

This decisive shift toward examining the representational codes of cinema was aided in particular by the influence of the British journal *Screen* and the growth in radical criticism of mainstream film. The writers who articulated these points most clearly in the 1970s were largely associated with film apparatus theory, which marked the first rigorous attempt to combine an analysis of the materiality of cinema with its architectonic and institutional effects. The main proponent of apparatus theory, Jean-Louis Baudry, like Gidal promoted a critical media practice and a distanced, critical mode of viewing that would demonstrate film's typically concealed ideological operations.[5] For these writers, the choice was simple and the implications profound: spectatorship was either complicit and immersed in the dominant ideology or, through critical and formal distance, was aware of and participating in an ideological critique formally and conceptually internal to the media work itself.

In the case of classic Hollywood cinema, apparatus theory seemed to provide a clear lens through which to conceptualize viewership and its ideological ramifications (although apparatus theory itself would come under increasing scrutiny within the discipline of film studies).[6] That the case is not so straightforward for screen-reliant installation has posed difficulties for art criticism. On the one hand, the introduction of media screens into sculptural installations in the late 1960s implicitly reintroduced illusionistic and virtual space into a type of art practice that, drawing on the critical ambitions of minimalism, had aimed to eliminate modernist transcendentalism in favor of a present-tense perceptual encounter between the spectator and the art object. On the other hand, in investigating the screen's material apparatus—even while incorporating virtual spaces into the work—certain projects produced a critical spectatorship characterized by a sort of doubleness that built upon yet differed from that presented by minimalism.[7] This mode of viewing was characterized by what art historian Michael Fried famously dubbed "theatricality," but only in part.[8] The hybrid status of screen-reliant installation spectatorship—both active and passive, material and immaterial—strained dominant critical models of the era, the critical prescriptions and political preoccupations of which proved to be unsuitable for addressing the particular critical interventions of this distinctive mode of art practice.[9]

As we shall see in what follows, by dispersing focus across screen spaces that coexist, and indeed sometimes compete with the actual exhibition space, certain media installations generate a forceful, critical effect that hinges precisely on this tension between illusionist/virtual and material/actual spaces. In a curious amalgamation of gallery-based spatial experimentation and political aesthetics, this model of spectatorship proposes that viewers be both "here" (embodied subjects in the material exhibition space) *and* "there" (observers looking onto screen spaces) in the here and now. In so doing, this new double spatial dynamic, staged as a bodily encounter in real time, radically reinterprets the conventional ways that technological screen interfaces have been described and experienced.

What a Difference a Screen Makes

Evaluating theories of screen-mediated spectatorship seems a logical starting point in assessing the influence of screens upon the spatial dynamics of media art viewing. Media scholars Anne Friedberg and Lev Manovich (both working outside the boundaries of a strictly art historical context) offer the two most compelling accounts of the screen's ambiguous material and discursive formations. Specifically focusing on the continuities and distortions enabled by film, video, and computer screens, both writers emphasize our cultural tendency to view flat pictorial surfaces from canvases to computer screens as "windows onto other worlds" and note how the Renaissance model of perspectival illusionism (outlined in Alberti's 1435 treatise "Della Pittura") has conditioned Western perceptions of spaces on flat surfaces ever since.

In *The Virtual Window,* Friedberg explores how the screen's role as a component piece of architecture has dramatically changed the materiality of built space.[10] While her primary focus is on the film screen, Friedberg's innovation is to recognize how the screen's immaterial architecture (its virtual space) informs and reflects an architecture of viewing. In the case of cinema, this means that the screen traditionally frames a view of a space that is conceptually, though not literally, distinct from the viewer's material space. In *The Language of New Media,* Manovich offers a three-part typology of screen viewing experiences, from the Renaissance to the present, based upon the viewer's physical and conceptual relationship to representational space, making further distinctions among viewing regimes in terms of temporality, scale, and levels of "interactivity."[11] Manovich's typology, in establishing the ways in which viewing moving, illuminated images on a media screen (characteristics he associates with "dynamic" and "real time" screen traditions) is qualitatively different from viewing illusionist imagery painted on canvas (what he calls the "classical" screen tradition), implicitly demonstrates that media screen viewing necessitates its own discrete critical framework.

Evaluating the spatial conditions of screen spectatorship in terms of everyday viewing experiences with commercial media technologies, Friedberg and Manovich devote comparatively little attention to alternate modes of engagement, including the ways in which certain media artworks create and reflect atypical viewing experiences. Redeploying mass media screens in art gallery installations, artists have created what one might call "warped" spaces—virtual and actual screen-based spaces that transform the spatial dynamics of art and media spectatorship.[12] Possible specifically screen-reliant spaces proposed and presented in media installation are many and complex, including but not limited to the space inside the screen (the screen acts as a window onto a space of representation); the space in front of or before the screen (the screen is used in a way that draws attention to the space between the viewer and the screen); and the real spatial presence of the frequently overlooked screen itself as an object.

Theories of identification and suture from film studies, typically worked out within a psychoanalytic framework, have carefully analyzed the spatialized interchange between the film screen and spectator. Writers such as Christian Metz and Laura Mulvey, for instance, have proposed a sort of spectatorial doubleness in which the space separating subject and screen must be forgotten but also maintained.[13] The doubleness I propose in regard to media installation is different in two key respects. First, whereas these film theories arose in relationship to moving images tied to narrative cinema (which privileges time), media installation, crucially, is tied more to space. Whereas cinema viewers are conventionally expected to disregard actual space and time for the duration of the film, the media artworks examined in this chapter insistently push their viewers to be mindful of the material exhibition space (as experienced in "real" time). Second, screen-reliant installations, in contrast to mainstream narrative cinema, privilege the material apparatus: the viewer's experience with these works foregrounds not only the space between the viewer and screen, but also the space of the (usually overlooked) technological media object itself.[14] The screen shifts from being the apex of the viewer's "cone" of vision (centering the viewer as in perspectival painting) to being a conceptual and literal point of emphasis that the viewer moves *around* (something closer to minimalist sculpture).

Seeing Double: "A Film to Play, A Film to Be Played"

Among the critical media projects in the late 1960s and early 1970s that emphasized not only the space(s) represented "inside" or "on" the screen, but also, crucially, the space in front of the screen and the space occupied by the material screen object itself, two artworks by VALIE EXPORT and Peter Campus respectively stand out as particularly useful explorations of the excessive and resistant capacities of screen interfaces. As the evocative titles *Ping Pong* (EXPORT, 1968) and *Interface* (Campus, 1972) suggest, these projects expressly interrogate screen spaces and screen-reliant visuality as part of the work. *Ping Pong* and *Interface* are distinguished by being among the first works to be specifically interested in the spatial dynamics of media spectatorship in relation to art spectatorship, and both provide clear examples of the particular kind of critical spectatorial doubling and displacement made possible with this mode of art practice.

Created in 1968, EXPORT's film installation *Ping Pong* consists of a commercial Ping-Pong ball, a paddle, and one-half of a full-sized Ping-Pong table abutted against a white wall. A black-and-white 8 mm film is projected onto the wall/screen from a low position at the back of the dimly lit room, regularly churning out unremarkable images of large black dots, which slowly appear and disappear in an alternating rhythm over the course of the film's three-minute duration. Merging haptic and optic experience, the work invites viewers to play Ping-Pong against these moving targets. The subtitle EXPORT occasionally uses to describe the piece—"Ein Film zum Spielen, ein Spielfilm" (A Film to [Be] Play[ed])—highlights the spectator's role in "completing" the work. Further, because the film is projected from the back of the room, the spectator's shadow appears on the wall/screen, becoming part of the screen space, collapsing any distinction between the viewer and the viewed.

In comparison to the "prepared" Ping-Pong paddles created by Fluxus artist George Maciunas in 1965–66, in which commercial paddles were subjected to a range of humorous modifications (including convex, hinged, or hollow surfaces, some subsequently put to use in a playful Fluxus "Olympics"), EXPORT's work is significantly more perverse. In a seemingly generous gesture, one conceptually similar to Bruce Nauman's participatory corridor works realized between 1969 and 1972, EXPORT's *Ping Pong* invites its spectator to partake in a game, but the very terms of engagement—a befuddled viewer struggling to hit a predetermined series of flickering projected circles even while his/her shadow interferes with the process—ensure that the viewer/player will emerge neither satisfied nor victorious.[15]

It is in part the anxiety and frustration central to *Ping Pong*'s game that triggers the work's critical effect.[16] Urging her spectators to pick up a paddle and play "against" an imaginary screen-based opponent, EXPORT arguably proposes the screen itself as a subject whose action is both represented by projected images and embodied in the materiality of the blank wall. Hitting the screen with the Ping-Pong ball, however, renders the screen a material object and, at least momentarily, cancels any implication of depth. Prefiguring Michael Snow's influential film installation *Two Sides to Every Story* (1974), in which two versions of a single film are projected onto opposite sides of a thin, rectangular aluminum screen, EXPORT uses opacity and transparency as conceptual tools to deny entry into the image space. That EXPORT's projection screen is an impassable gallery wall, and therefore

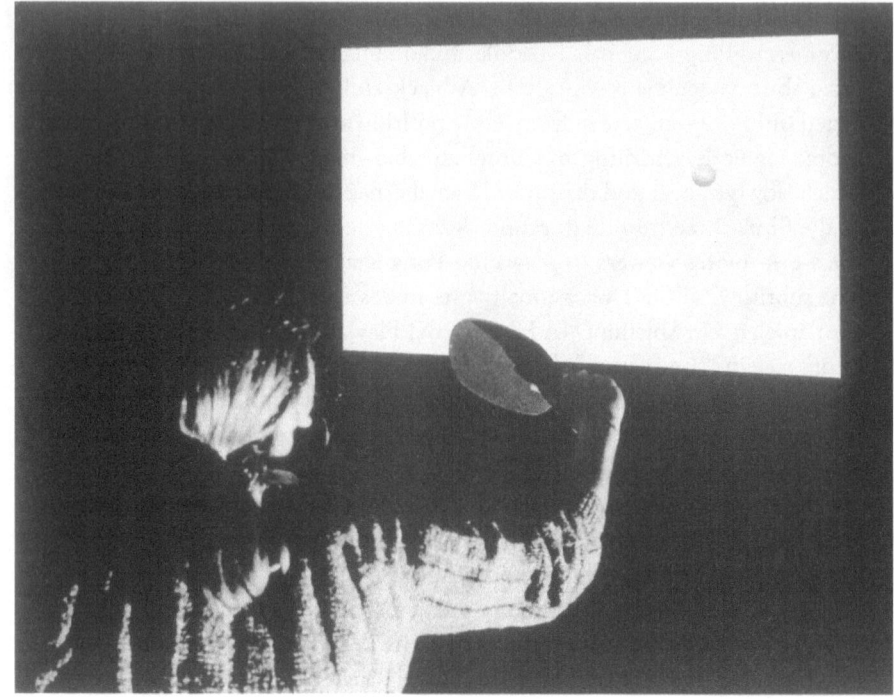

VALIE EXPORT, *Ping Pong,* 1968. 8 mm black-and-white film, silent, solid screen, table tennis rackets, Ping-Pong balls; 3 minutes (loop). Installation view of spectator "playing" Ping-Pong against the screen-based opponent. Archive VALIE EXPORT. Photograph by Werner Mraz. Courtesy of Generali Foundation Collection, Vienna.

indisputably material, makes it even more clear that the artist intended for her spectator to take note of the physical installation space even while engrossed in the screen's immaterial, illusionist content.[17] *Ping Pong*'s relentless insistence on depth and surface, immateriality and materiality, productively draws the viewer's attention to the correlation between these multiple spaces.

EXPORT's imaginary yet actual Ping-Pong game insistently tests the normative spatiality of screen spectatorship, conceptually and literally fusing the spectator and the spectacle. In the single screen of EXPORT's work, conflicting spaces are mobilized and experienced simultaneously: the spectator's opponent is imagined "inside" the illusionary screen space and yet the game actually takes place in real space and depends upon the recogni-

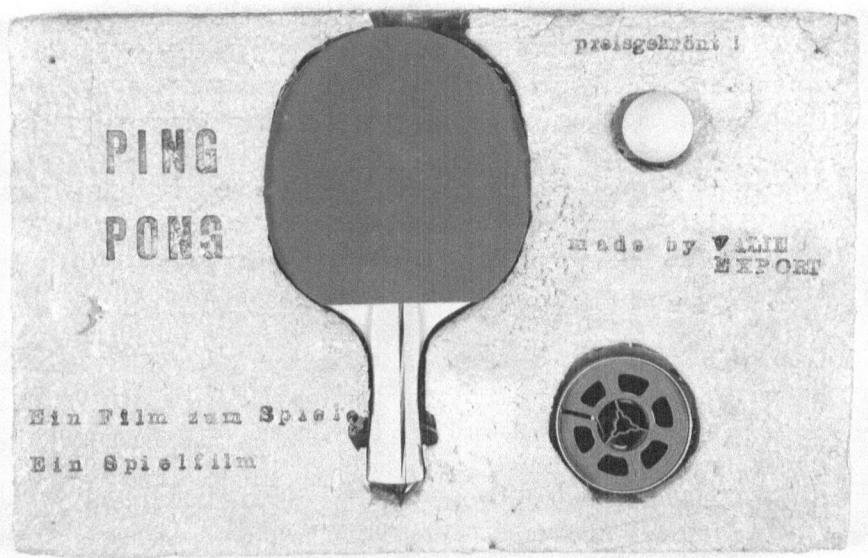

VALIE EXPORT, *Ping Pong Kassette,* 1968. Polystyrene object, stamp imprint, aluminum foil, table tennis racket, ball, 8 mm film, 31 x 48 x 3.5 cm. VALIE EXPORT advertised a do-it-yourself, ready-made version of her *Ping Pong* installation that included a ball, paddle, and 8 mm film (the consumer presumably supplied projector and screen). Copyright Generali Foundation Collection. Photograph by Werner Kaligofsky.

tion and use of the screen as a physical object. The immaterial dots of projected light that the spectator gamely endeavors to hit look like targets emerging from inside or beyond the screen (the projected image of the ball must be imagined as a quasi-real object for the game to work). At the same time, the actual ball's automatic return bouncing off the screen and back to the spectator confirms both the screen's material flatness (rivaling the screen's other, generally starring role as a window onto a space of illusionist representation) and the actuality of the spectator's embodied experience in the gallery space.

In this manner, *Ping Pong* exploits the screen's duality as material and immaterial to draw attention to the typically neglected space *in front of* the screen—that is to say, the space between the screen object and its viewer. Put another way, *Ping Pong* proposes an oppositional viewing space within a space. The movement of the real Ping-Pong ball—its route from the viewer's space to the screen space and back again—materializes the neglected circuit between body and screen. In this way it serves as a metaphor for the intellectual work EXPORT expects her spectator to perform. The artist has written about her ambitions for this piece vis-à-vis theatrical cinema spectatorship: "*Ping Pong* explains the relationship of domination between the producer (the director) and the consumer (the spectator). What the eye tells the brain is the cause for motoric *[sic]* reflexes and reactions. Spectators and screen are the screen for a game with rules that are dictated by the director. Attempt to emancipate the audience!"[18]

At first read—"Attempt to emancipate the audience!"—it would seem that the artist hopes to free spectators from the constraints of passive media viewing by insisting that they, as Ping-Pong players, become active viewers/participants—a somewhat paradoxical ambition that was nonetheless inspirational for many artists at the time.[19] Indeed, a Brechtian influence is unmistakable in EXPORT's rallying cry. Brecht considered the "apparatus" to be a field of signification including the technical tools, the cultural institutions, and the parties in control of those institutions. Providing a foundation for subsequent developments in film theory, he contended that disruption of the unitary field presented by the apparatus would make spectators inherently self-aware.[20]

EXPORT's *Ping Pong* changes this relationship slightly. As the artist explains, spectators and screen "are the screen" for an additional "game." The viewers and screen in EXPORT's game are the site of a further strategic intervention, one whose rules are, tellingly, "dictated by the director." If the first game is the table tennis match between the viewer and the screen-cum-opponent, the second game is one staged between the omnipotent director and the active yet passive viewer whose participation is entirely prescripted. What would otherwise seem to be the straightforward emancipatory potential of EXPORT's invitation for viewers to become active participants with her film is thus corrupted from the outset. The organizing logic of *Ping Pong* is not so much the liberatory potential of revealing the apparatus as it is a pointed critique of cinematic spectatorship via the multiplication and complication of the spatial conditions for experiencing screen interfaces.

By asking viewers to play a "real" game centered on a "virtual" projected image, EXPORT offers spectators the possibility to consider simultaneously the space of the screen's immaterial representation (the projected ball) and its relationship to the material world (the viewer's actual Ping-

Pong game in the exhibition space). Further, by visually incorporating the viewer's body into the representational screen space in the form of the viewer's shadow, EXPORT's installation emphasizes the conventionally obscured connections between viewer, material exhibition space, and immaterial screen space. In its insistent and evident critique of cinematic spectatorship (for the record, it won the award for the "most political film" at the Viennese Film Festival in 1968), *Ping Pong* exemplifies the way in which on-screen visual information in a media installation may be less significant than the manipulations of the conventional spatial dynamics associated with screen-based spectatorship.

Embodiment at the Interface

Equally unflinching in its attempt to undermine the viewer's seemingly disembodied relationship to screen-reliant spaces, and sharing *Ping Pong's* minimalist aesthetic, Peter Campus's closed-circuit video installation *Interface* (1972) nonetheless stages a wholly different experience for its viewer. Entering the darkened gallery, viewers encounter a nearly empty room punctuated by a video projector and camera placed at opposite ends of the gallery, approximately twelve feet apart. A large (six foot by eight foot) transparent glass screen, unobtrusive but immediately identifiable in the relatively empty gallery, divides the exhibition space, separating the ground-level light source and projector from the video camera stationed at the wall opposite.

As viewers move through the gallery and step into the space in front of the glass, two simultaneous, full-length images of themselves appear on it: their reflected mirror image coupled with their live video image (captured by the camera from behind the glass). While negotiating a path between the conspicuous obstacles of the camera, projector, and screen, Campus's spectator enjoys the ability to influence what is represented on the glass screen. Depending on where one stands in the gallery space, the two near-life-size likenesses can appear spatially superimposed or side by side, presenting viewers with an uncanny dual portrait of simultaneous yet dissimilar self-images. While many artists working with video in the 1970s would exploit the medium's capacity for depicting parallel time, taking advantage of video's ability to depict an electronically mediated present concomitant with the viewer's real-time experience in the gallery space, the particular way in which *Interface* troubles the representations of its viewers foregrounds the oft-neglected materiality of the body–screen interface. Like the screen-centric and screen-directed Ping-Pong game in EXPORT's installation,

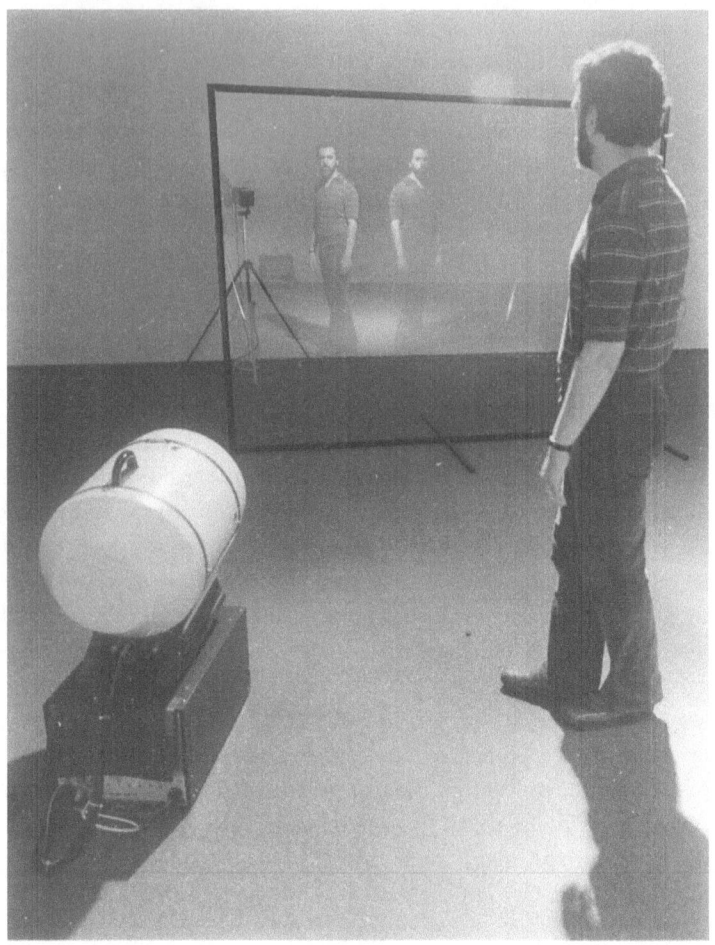

Peter Campus, *Interface,* 1972. Installation view of projector,
glass screen, and camera, showing a spectator's dual
reflected and projected images. Courtesy of Locks Gallery,
Philadelphia, Pennsylvania.

Interface creates an awareness in the viewer of the screen's role in conceptually and physically mediating (manipulating) relations between itself,
the projection, and the viewer.

Both *Interface* and *Ping Pong* call attention to the spatial presence of
the material screen object, but in such a way as to underscore that a screen
is a performative category: nearly any object can temporarily function as a

Interface

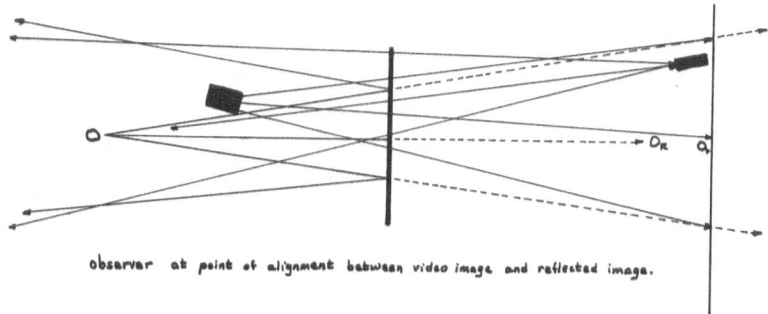

observer at point of alignment between video image and reflected image.

The plane of tangency between
reflected space and video space.
Postulation that at least these
three spaces coexist.

Peter Campus, _Interface_, 1972. Artist's diagram depicting the
spatialized arrangement between camera, monitor, observer,
glass screen, and the related feedback imagery. Courtesy of
Locks Gallery, Philadelphia, Pennsylvania.

screen under precisely specified conditions. By projecting images onto a
sheet of glass (Campus) or a gallery wall (EXPORT), these works of art
point to the way in which virtually anything can be reconfigured as a screen
and thus act as a window onto another space. In the case of Campus's _Inter-
face,_ the transparency of the glass reveals the relative opacity of the image;
in a strange reversal, light emerges as matter. Put slightly differently, Campus's screen must nearly disappear in order to (re)materialize the interface
of screen-based viewing.

Analyzing the spectatorial address of Campus's video installations alongside others made by Graham and Nauman in the 1970s, art historian
David Joselit proposes that the critical relevance of these works is the way
in which they destabilize normative television spectatorship. In his "The
Video Public Sphere," Joselit points out how the subversive and defamiliar-
izing spatial experience central to these installations serves to render explicit
the "idealized identifications" between viewers and fictional characters of
highly moralized fictional TV narratives.[21] While I agree that mass media
spectatorship is central to the viewer's experience with video art, and indeed

to the spectatorship of any media art, *Interface* opens the possibility for critical reflection on conditions of mediated viewing that extend beyond specular identification with commercial television to contemporary subjectivity more generally.

Interface's translucent glass is both metaphorically and materially linked to a window. Yet this material form works to question the screen's typical role as interface between the real and the virtual and to highlight the way in which screens usually operate as literal and conceptual barriers, offering spectators a facade of autonomous disengagement from the "other side." While Campus clearly intended for spectators to view the glass from the side that would generate their double likeness, it is nonetheless *possible* to observe this screen from both sides. Viewers can look at this screen as a virtual window but can also look *through* it, from "behind." Because spectators can view it from all sides, they are able to understand Campus's screen as an arbitrary division (or, perhaps more accurately, an arbitrary pocket of virtual space) inside the real exhibition space.

Campus's choice of projection surface emphatically confirms that *both* sides of the media screen exist in real space, available for the viewer's exploration and potential intervention. *Interface* enables visual *continuity* in terms of the spectator's spatial perception, thereby destabilizing the screen's conventional role of depicting representations that are visually and/or conceptually *discontinuous* with the spectator's own space. This reversal is profound inasmuch as it challenges our traditional experiences with both screen space and real, material space in an art context. Accustomed to granting visual priority to media screens and to viewing screens as windows onto other spaces, viewers initially train their attention to the representational space "inside" Campus's glass screen. Confronted with two different yet simultaneous self-images — closed-circuit video and mirror images that continuously transform as viewers walk around the exhibition space — viewers are incited to question the representational integrity of screen spaces. This questioning in turn compels the spectator to contemplate the physical gallery space in conjunction with (and as related to) the representational screen space. Exceeding dominant models proposed in both art and film/media criticism in the expanded field of film and art practices in the 1960s and 1970s — which tended to see media installations as either process-based attempts to disrupt illusionist space with "real" space or as materialist interventions against the "bad ideal" of conventional mainstream cinema — *Interface*'s forceful critical effect hinges upon its insistent attention to (as

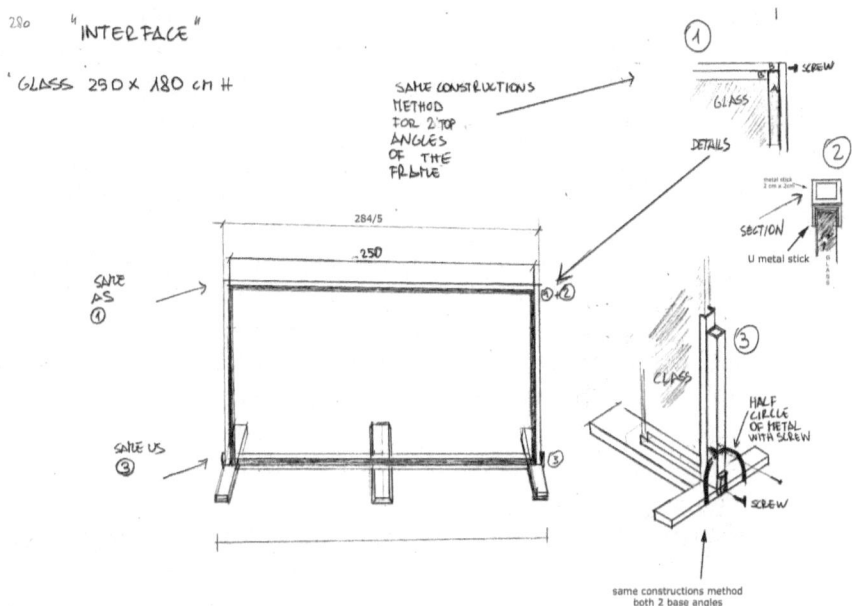

Drawing of Peter Campus's *Interface*, 1972. Designer Antonio
Trimani's sketch of the glass frame constructed for *Interface*
in the exhibition "Zero Visibility," Genezzano, Italy, 2001.
Courtesy of Locks Gallery, Philadelphia, Pennsylvania.

opposed to rejection of) illusionist, virtual space. Like the material yet immaterial screen itself, real space and illusionist space are revealed to be coterminous.

Walking around the installation, viewers can appreciate Campus's "screen" for what it is: the minimal flat surface required for mediation between the viewer and the informational or representational space seemingly inside the screen, a thin membrane that nonetheless customarily establishes a sort of boundary line defining outside versus inside, actual versus virtual. While media screens may typically presume and reinforce a degree of disengagement between the times and spaces inside and in front of the screen (often encouraging attention to the former at the expense of the latter), the potentially radical intervention of works such as Campus's *Interface* and EXPORT's *Ping Pong* is how they ask their spectators to remain fully present in *both* temporal and spatial realms. These works propose a self-consciously dual spectatorship—one simultaneously caught up in the space of illusionist representation *and* made aware of the material conditions of the viewing experience. While spectators are allowed to partially immerse themselves in illusionist, virtual times and spaces, they must concurrently recognize their embodied presence in the here and now of the exhibition space.

Interface's reflected and projected images emphasize this twofold aspect of embodied media viewing. Spectators readily comprehend the most obvious difference between their two likenesses represented in *Interface* because the viewer's mirror reflection appears in color, whereas the slightly hazier video image appears in black-and-white. However, the work generates an interesting perceptual riddle beyond this difference. The viewer's image, like all mirror reflections, appears in reverse, while the comparatively ghostly black-and-white video image shows the viewer the "right" way, perfectly imitating the viewer's posture and body orientation. If the viewer stretches out his or her right arm, for example, the screen reveals a video image of a figure stretching his or her right arm, whereas the (inverted) mirrored image appears to stretch the left arm in relationship to the screen's implied interior space. This discrepancy generates an unexpected, and therefore dramatic, effect: the slightly fainter black-and-white video image that perfectly mimics one's body's posture in relationship to the gallery space can appear more "real." Mediated reality—the uncanny image of one's self from without—assumes a primary importance as *Interface*'s spectators struggle to regain their sense of embodied self. The projected video portrait thus allows Campus's viewer a disconcerting glimpse into how he or she is seen by others.

Film theory provides one tool with which to approach this phenomenon. Indeed, the spectator constructed in *Interface* is closely related to the Lacanian notion of the subject founded in (mediated) vision.[22] Baudry's 1970 essay regarding the ideological effects of the cinema had drawn explicitly on Lacan's theorization of the mirror stage, which proposed a model of subjectivity as a fusion of the viewer and the viewed (displacing the notion of a stable, coherent Cartesian subject). The Lacanian subject, "caught up in the lure of spatial identification," passes through a stage in which an external (mirror) image of the body allows the subject to identify itself, albeit erroneously, as a unified "I"—as a subject.[23] This initial misrecognition has long-term psychic effects, generating a sort of doubled and contingent subjectivity fundamentally dependent upon its imaging by *external* objects and an "other," as Campus's *Interface*, with its concurrent mirror and video images of the viewer, effectively demonstrates.

The disquieting existence of two simultaneous yet different self-images is only part of the labyrinth of screen-reliant spaces Campus's spectator is asked to reconcile. *Interface* initially exploits the spectator's habitual screen-as-window viewing techniques, expecting its viewer to immediately understand the glass "screen" as a threshold to another representational space and to train his or her attention on the information or images being presented "inside" the screen space, on the "other side" of the glass. And yet, by presenting viewers with divergent live images of their own bodies, and by making the camera and projector technology visible and accessible, *Interface* compels its viewers to consider the space *in front of* the screen—the media(ted) space between the viewer and the screen—in addition to, and as coextensive with, the representational space *inside* the screen. It is only by understanding their role as embodied observers in the exhibition space, understanding the reciprocal relationship between their body placement, the projector, camera, and screen, that Campus's spectators can unlock the riddle of their dissimilar live images.

What is important to stress is the way in which Campus's installation establishes how the viewing techniques allegedly associated with mainstream media forms and self-reflexive, embodied spectatorship are not mutually exclusive. Like *Ping Pong, Interface* proposes a spectator whose experiences with a range of screen spaces serve to confirm, rather than usurp or render secondary, his or her experiences in the material here and now of the exhibition space. In an apparent contradiction, *Interface* generates an embodied spectatorship by asking spectators to engage with virtual screen space. Simultaneously engaging actual *and* virtual space, materiality *and* immateriality, this critical model of spectatorial doubleness effectively destabilizes conventional binary distinctions between these seemingly discrete categories.

EXPORT's *Ping Pong* and Campus's *Interface* provide cogent historical examples of the radical potential for certain media art configurations to productively destabilize our conventional relationships to screen spaces.[24] They also provide, like the other projected and moving-image installations assessed thus far, provocative models for thinking about contemporary screen-mediated subjectivity. Both works offer potentially disorienting temporal and physical displacements, yet in both, the viewing experience is effectively rendered in an embodied present—by the viewer's erratic optical and physical engagement with the prerecorded footage in *Ping Pong* and by his or her disorienting encounter with the closed-circuit loop of *Interface.* By foregrounding an active relationship between the spectator, media objects, exhibition space, and screen spaces, these media art installations generate a self-conscious and troubled spectatorship explicitly contingent upon the articulated tension between actual and virtual times and spaces. We are simultaneously both here *and* there, both now *and* then.

Taking the viewer's relationship to screen space as their very subject matter, both *Ping Pong* and *Interface* work to reveal the institutional and ideological implications of the mass media spectator's tendency to focus on the image or other information "inside" the screen and, in so doing, to effectively divorce the image space from their own space. These sculptural environments ask their audiences to consider the implications of their physically embodied and subjectively disembodied relation to these media interfaces: not only do spectators see themselves seeing in *Ping Pong* and *Interface,* they are viscerally and unremittingly reminded of the embodied conditions of *all* media viewing. In the next chapter's analysis of art environments that incorporate computer screen interfaces, we shall see that this can also be conceived as an ethical issue and as a challenge to key premises of art, film, and media spectatorship as they conventionally have been understood.

Turning to the topic of computer screens in chapter 5, I begin by posing a similar inquiry into the spatial dynamics of spectatorship. How do computer screen-reliant artworks negotiate spectatorial doubleness and to what critical effect? Are we, as spectators of new media art installations, both here *and* there—or, perhaps more ominously, are we neither fully here *nor* there?

5. What Lies Ahead
Virtuality, the Body, and the Computer Screen

*One must look at a display screen as a window through which one beholds a
virtual world. The challenge to computer graphics is to make the picture in the
window look real, sound real, and the objects act real.*

— IVAN SUTHERLAND, "The Ultimate Display" (1965)

*Today it is the very space of habitation that is conceived as both receiver and
distributor, as the space of both reception and operations, the control screen and
terminal which as such may be endowed with telematic power — that is, with
the capability of regulating everything from a distance, including work,
consumption, play, social relations, and leisure.*

— JEAN BAUDRILLARD, The *Ecstasy of
Communication* (1987)

Computer science prodigy Ivan Sutherland's prescription for the "ultimate
display" in 1965 came down firmly on the side of representational illusionism. The computer screen should function as an Albertian window: a
flat surface through which to behold simulated, virtual spaces. Only two
decades later, sociologist and philosopher Jean Baudrillard diagnosed a situation in which virtual screen-based spaces appeared poised to become the
primary sites for mediating between real world environments. The transformation from Sutherland's seemingly audacious proposition to develop
virtual screen-based environments to the acknowledgment of computer-
mediated telepresence and teleaction between *actual* environments is a
dramatic one.[1] Both thinkers' remarks, however, prove remarkably prophetic
for theorizing screen-reliant art spectatorship in our digital age. Recent
graphical human-computer interfaces treat the computer screen as both a

virtual window (a site for representation) *and* a virtual instrument panel (a tool for manipulating external reality). A markedly new mode of experiencing screen spaces emerges in the process.

This chapter's goal is to extend chapter 4's examination of the spatial dynamics of viewing screen-reliant art objects by specifically focusing on installations conceived and executed with digital computer screens.[2] At first blush, one might argue that there is nothing categorically distinct about the viewer's encounter with such works; after all, this book has already identified a vast and indeterminate territory between the viewer and the viewed, between real and virtual spaces, in art environments employing film and video. These participatory, experiential sculptures investigate the interpenetration between the space "on" the screen, the space between the viewer and the screen, and the space of the screen object itself. Closed-circuit video works depicted real-time views of spaces geographically removed from the viewer's own space well before the introduction of networked computer technologies, and other two-dimensional representations, such as perspectival systems, maps, and x-rays, have unquestionably been employed to affect reality from a distance before the development of digital media.[3] Any fervent assertions about the novelty of the "interactivity" or "virtuality" that are commonly attributed to digital art should therefore ring hollow. Nevertheless, the spaces of screen-reliant art spectatorship have indeed multiplied alongside changes in media technologies, and it is important to train a critical eye on them so that their artistic potential and liability might be better understood.[4] As we shall see, with the new spatial relationships enabled by digital computer networks comes a complex and potentially destabilizing type of viewership, one characterized by both radically new screen-based powers and profound spatial uncertainties for viewing subjects.

Electronic telecommunications enable the instantaneous transmission of images; when used in conjunction with screen-reliant media technologies, they can also facilitate real-time remote control. These technological developments make it possible for computer-based artworks to link not only the viewer's physical space with the representational environments conceptualized as "inside" or on the screen, but also, and more profoundly, to engender (tele)presence and action between these two realms and *actual* remote locales. That is, spectators can use images to manipulate all kinds of resources from a distance and in real time. This is not merely an issue of being psychologically involved with the narrative or images on screen or even of acknowledging the structuring role of the screen-based apparatus, but rather of using a real-time representational media environment to act in a different place altogether.[5]

The consequences for media art spectatorship are especially noteworthy: there are subjective effects to being in many places simultaneously. Art and media historian Oliver Grau specifically emphasizes the computer screen's role in this transition. He argues that telepresence and teleaction enable the user to be present in three places at the same time: "(a) in the spatio-temporal location determined by the user's body; (b) by means of *teleperception* in the simulated, virtual image space; and (c) by means of *teleaction* in the place where, for example, a robot is situated, directed by one's own movements and providing orientation through its sensors."[6] Film and media scholar Anne Friedberg confirms that viewing subjects inhabit a "fractured, post-Cartesian cyberspace [and] cybertime" in their experience with certain new media technologies. "On the computer, we can be two (or more) places at once, in two (or more) time frames, in two (or more) modes of identity," she observes.[7] In proposing that the subject's relationship with digital computing does away with any remaining shards of spatial located-ness, Grau and Friedberg reinforce a now familiar critique of the postmodern condition from Jameson to Baudrillard. What I'd like to emphasize here, however, is how the computer screen's new connective possibilities further a tension of spectatorship considered in the previous chapter: the tug-of-war between being "both here *and* there"—psychologically and physically invested simultaneously in the physical gallery space and in screen spaces—and being "neither here *nor* there"—being overcome by so many screen-reliant spaces as to be effectively prevented from being consciously present in any of them.

Two celebrated new media works, Lynn Hershman's *The Difference Engine #3* (1995–98) and Ken Goldberg's *The Telegarden* (1995–2004), can help us to recognize and theorize the critical import of these changed spatial relationships. Both of these complicated, engineering-intensive media art projects were immediately recognized for their pioneering efforts: *The Difference Engine #3* won the prestigious Golden Nica Award at Ars Electronica in 1999 and *The Telegarden* was awarded the top prize at the Festival for Interactive Arts and the Kobe Award at the Interactive Media Festival in 1995.[8] Art historians and critics, however, have been slow to tackle the thorny issues that works such as these raise about new media art's relationship to digital communication technologies. This is due at least in part to the fact that both pieces are arguably more compelling as conceptual thought experiments than as either functional environments or elegantly executed artworks in their own right. These multisited art objects, operating both inside and outside the physical confines of art institutions, are nevertheless exemplary for opening new ways in which to explore the sites associated with experiencing screen-reliant art. In so doing they also reveal an enormous amount about prospective interactions between viewers and digital screens.

Inasmuch as the real-time electronic transmission of signals and information enables telepresence and teleaction—the ability to be functionally present and/or to act at a location other than one's physical location—it constitutes a crucial epistemological break in the arena of viewer-screen interactions. This momentous shift allows the viewing subject to have power over not just the simulation on the screen, but *over material reality itself.* While telecombat and telesurgery are two of the most striking examples, artistic applications, from live Web surveillance cameras interspersed with footage of professional actors (Diller and Scofidio) to remote-control gardening (Ken Goldberg), are equally radical, at least on a conceptual level.[9] Although the visual arts have long been concerned with the creation of and engagement with virtual, simulated worlds, computer-based installations now up the ante, precisely by enabling active, operational connections to actual remote environments.[10] Moreover, the digital screen's "remote control" activity is potentially bidirectional: every networked viewing environment is potentially subject to being observed and/or acted upon and is also subject to the appearance of simulations. Not every encounter with a computer screen will necessarily make changes in a distant material environment, of course, nor will the viewer's space automatically be compromised by actions from afar. These very possibilities, however, definitively change the viewing subject's relationship to computer screen interfaces. In this way, the largely unprecedented spatial dynamics between the viewer and artworks reliant on digital screens raise a host of timely ethical questions in our so-called virtual era, even above and beyond their transitional role for art spectatorship. What is the nature of the screen-based action and communication between subjects in distant but networked environments? How does one know for certain whether a screen-based site is linked to a "real" physical place? If one can't be sure, how might key phenomenological conditions concerning embodiment, mobility, and even one's sense of subjective identity change?

Two-Way Mirror Power

The Difference Engine #3 is a multisited art work that joins a "real world" sculptural installation at the ZKM | Center for Art and Media (Karlsruhe, Germany) to an immaterial, screen-based environment.[11] These elements are in turn connected to remote viewing stations via the Internet. Thus, the piece operates concurrently at multiple sites—online and throughout the ZKM museum—with up to forty-five multiple users at any given time. The portion housed in the ZKM comprises computer equipment, digital cameras, and a series of screens dispersed throughout the exhibition galleries. A large display screen greets visitors at the museum's entrance and three smaller bidirectional browsing units (BBUs) are stationed on pedestals at various points throughout the institution.

The BBU screens display graphical, perspectival renderings of the physical museum interior to visitors so that, as in many of the media installations examined thus far, the space inside the monitor depicts the actual gallery space surrounding it. Museum visitors are encouraged to tilt or rotate the BBUs to observe different computer-rendered viewpoints and perspectives inside the museum.[12] Equipped with sensors and digital cameras, the units are indeed "bidirectional"; they enable spectators to observe digital renderings of the museum interior even while the museumgoers themselves are being "observed" via the same devices. Courtesy of the attached cameras, the BBUs capture images of whatever (or whoever) is in front of them.

When a museum visitor approaches any of Hershman's three BBUs, a digital camera indiscernibly captures an image of that person and immediately feeds it into a part of the installation the artist dubs the "avatar archive." (An avatar is a graphical representation of a person within a virtual environment, often used to manipulate information or to navigate through virtual spaces.) Digital avatars of the museum visitors stream through the circuits of Hershman's sprawling sculpture, periodically appearing on the various display screens and BBU monitors dispersed throughout the museum. While many media installations incorporate spectators' images into the work itself (such as Bruce Nauman's video corridors or Peter Campus's *Interface*), *The Difference Engine #3* differs in the way that the spectators' images go on to become independent entities; the visitors' avatars are stored in perpetuity online, as part of an ever-expanding database in the work's virtual, screen-based environment.[13]

Hershman exploits the connectivity of the Internet to allow *The Difference Engine #3*'s remote online viewers to observe the same computer-

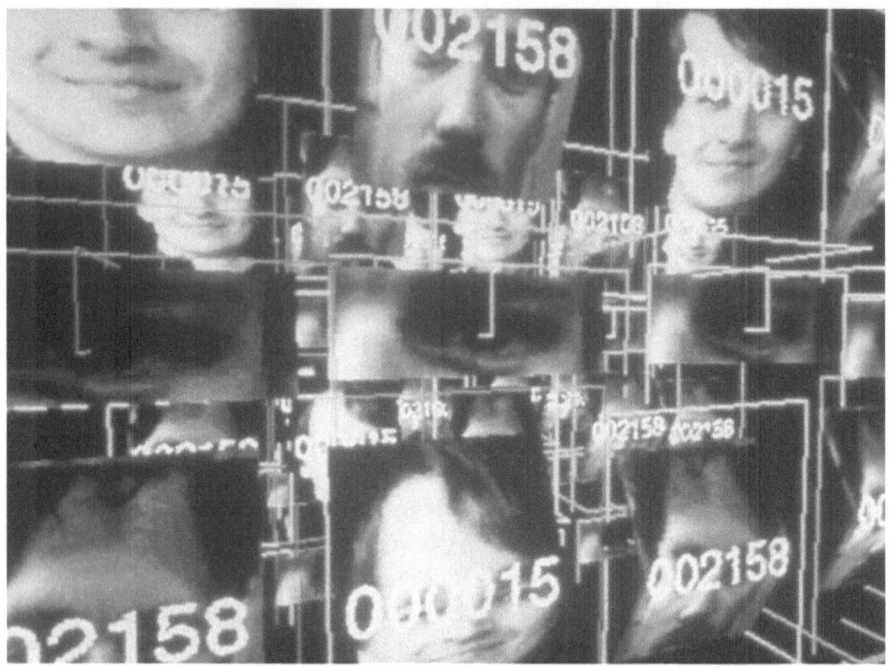

Lynn Hershman, *Difference Engine #3*, 1995–98. Screen shot view of the "avatar archive" component of this multisited new media installation. Courtesy of Lynn Hershman Leeson. Collection of ZKM | Center for Art and Media, Karlsruhe, Germany.

rendered views of the ZKM museum on their personal computer screens that visitors are observing on the BBUs in the museum. That is, spectators simultaneously see the same computerized views on their screens whether they are virtually or literally inside the museum. Like the visitors to the brick-and-mortar museum, online viewers are granted the privilege of manipulating the BBUs, although, in this case, the action is telerobotic, carried out on the monitor via the user's keyboard and mouse. Empowering remote audiences to make changes in the actual museum has curious collateral effects. For example, the museum visitors are first made aware of the two-way connectivity of the BBUs when the screens appear to move independently. The boundaries between viewer and viewed become distressingly frayed at this moment: while it is one thing to project a (qualified) truth value onto a screen world, finding oneself literally connected to that world is quite another.

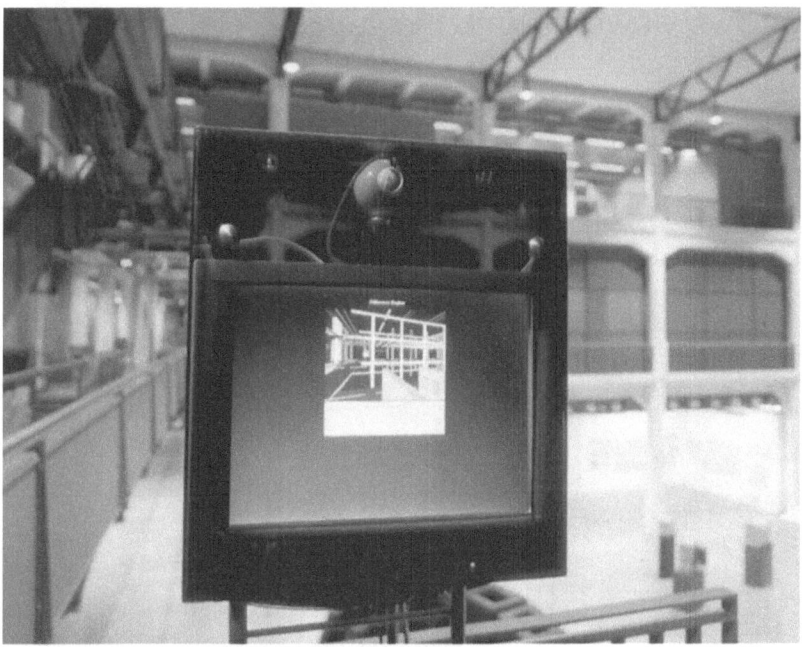

Lynn Hershman, *The Difference Engine #3*, 1995–98. Installation view depicting one of the artwork's "BBU" screens that
users can manipulate to observe different computer-rendered
viewpoints and perspectives inside the Karlsruhe museum.
Courtesy of Lynn Hershman Leeson. Collection of ZKM I Center
for Art and Media, Karlsruhe, Germany.

Significantly, one's degree of agency vis-à-vis panoptic manipulation is
further conditional upon where one encounters the piece. *The Difference
Engine #3* reveals sharp distinctions between the spectatorial experiences
of its two audiences—viewers who are physically in the museum and those
who access the work online. While viewers in the material museum are
unavoidably incorporated into Hershman's work in the form of their own
digital images-cum-avatars, online viewers navigate the piece by selecting
a "generic" avatar to represent them on their simulated journey through the
virtual ZKM museum. Visitors who physically enter the Karlsruhe museum
alternate the three BBU screen views by manually moving the monitors,
whereas online viewers change the imagery at the comparatively secluded
site of their PCs. Thus, while one group is automatically subject to external control mechanisms, the other has the relative luxury of deciding how
and to what degree they'd like to be implicated in the work. Put simply,

Two viewports into the same virtual space.

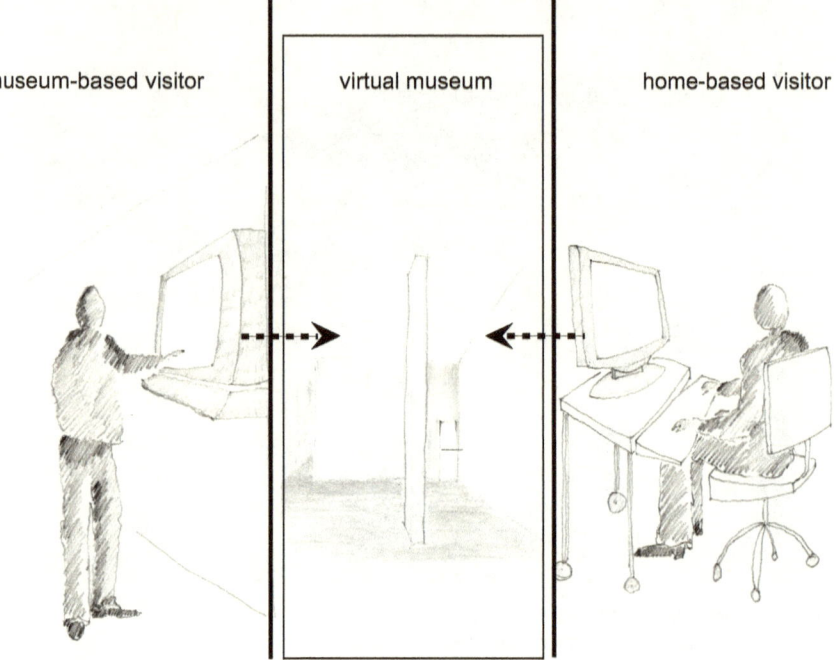

museum-based visitor   virtual museum   home-based visitor

Diagram of Lynn Hershman's *Difference Engine #3*. Drawing by Liska Chan, 2008. This diagram depicts the screen-based virtual space/site shared by the installation's remote and museum-based visitors that enables the work's two-way active connection. Note that remote visitors can manipulate screen objects (BBUs) located inside the actual Karlsruhe museum as well. Courtesy of Liska Chan.

viewers who engage Hershman's installation inside the ZKM building are physically vulnerable in a way that the dispersed online audience is not. Although in its current configuration *The Difference Engine #3* precludes the infliction of serious bodily harm on its viewers, it is not impossible to conceive of an interface being configured in such a way as to allow a remote observer to violently shift a BBU held by an unsuspecting museumgoer or to trigger a series of painful electric shocks for viewers on the "other side" of the screen.

Ken Goldberg's *The Telegarden* takes the as yet uncertain artistic promise of screen-based teleaction in a slightly different direction. The piece made its first appearance at the University of Southern California in 1995 before moving to the lobby of the Ars Electronica media art center in Linz, Austria, the following year. The museum component of the work consists of a small real-world garden, robotic gardening equipment, and an Internet-enabled PC that allows museum visitors to access the work's Web site. The Web site features more or less real-time images of the sometimes scraggly, sometimes lush garden taken from the perspective of a camera attached to the robotic arm. A schematic of the robot itself appears nearby and can be observed in tandem. Equipped with this visual information and detailed textual instructions, viewers can direct the robotic arm to plant and tend to a selection of petunias, peppers, eggplants, and marigolds. For the purposes of the present argument, it is important to recognize how, regardless of whether viewers encounter the installation in the museum or online, their ability to partake in tending the plot of earth is always screen-mediated. The closest they will get to touching garden soil is by manipulating pixilated images on their PC monitor.

Similar to *The Difference Engine #3*, multiple observers can interact with *The Telegarden* at the same time, regardless of their physical location. According to the artist, the ways in which members rely on each other to execute their remote gardening activities and nurture the physical plot on an ongoing basis is central to the meaning of the work itself.[14] For instance, the primary function of the "Alternate Village Square Chatroom"—an online discussion board located on the project's Web site—is to facilitate communication between the telegarden's computer users-cum-horticulturists.[15] This arrangement is also efficacious from a practical standpoint: the robotic interface can be hard for novices to understand without the help of other experienced users, and visitors—at least those keen on making the garden grow—must cooperate enough to avoid crushing each others' plants, over- or underwatering the soil, and so on.

As in Hershman's installation, not all spectators are granted equivalent opportunities for experiencing the work. The reasons for this discrepancy differ, however. *The Telegarden* incorporates a series of ingenious limits on viewer participation; users who officially register on the Web site are rewarded with greater opportunities for growing the garden as well as for collaborating and communicating with other gardeners.[16] Planting privileges are reserved for registered users, with further preference given to dedicated, repeat visitors. (For example, after 100 hits one is allocated a single seed, after 500 another seed, and a final seed at 1,000 hits.) Goldberg's decision to favor regular visitors is perhaps best explained in relationship to what media and architectural historian William J. Mitchell identifies as

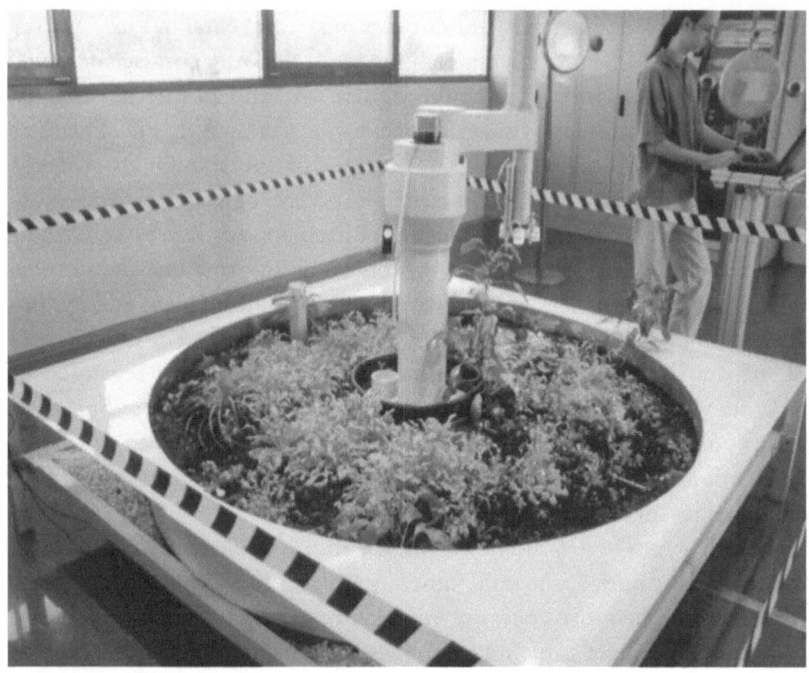

Ken Goldberg, *The Telegarden*, 1995–2004. Installation view of the real garden plot and robotic equipment at Ars Electronica media art center in Linz, Austria, comprising part of this multi-sited work. Courtesy of Ken Goldberg.

the phenomenon of "persistent" virtual spaces. Persistent virtual environments have many characteristics of successful brick-and-mortar architecture; that is, they "become increasingly familiar with repeated visits; seem to possess power to evoke memories of previous events that took place there [and] change and grow over time."[17] In the process of engaging such spaces, explains Mitchell, users are more likely to behave as they would when encountering a "real" place in person. He explains the conduct this way: "If you know that your environment will be there, as you left it, the next time you log in, then you have some motivation to invest time and resources in improving it. . . . If you realize that you will have to live with your fellow inhabitants for a long time, and that you will need them to respect and trust you, then you will be less tempted by role-playing and momentarily amusing deceptions."[18] In a seeming paradox, the more the spectators engage *The Telegarden*'s Web site as "real," the more they will treat the garden as such.

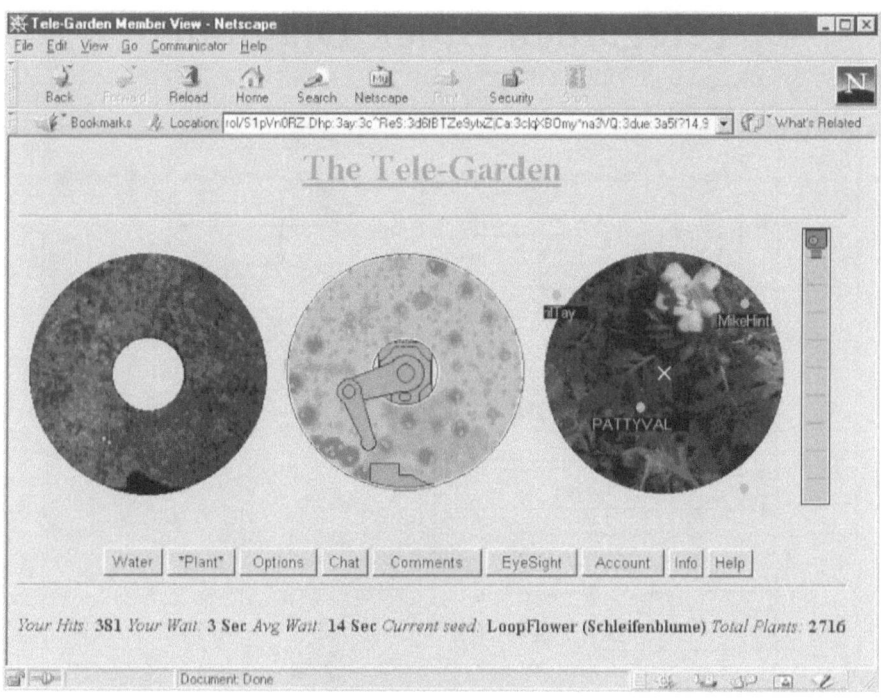

Ken Goldberg, *The Telegarden*, 1995–2004. Screen shot of
Internet-based component of Goldberg's installation depicting
views of a visitor's computer-screen-based remote gardening
activities. Courtesy of Ken Goldberg.

What is essential to note is that the spatial relationship between the
viewing subject and the screen is dramatically redefined in both artworks.
The telematic reach of Hershman's and Goldberg's installations demonstrates that the passivity of the so-called "virtual window" cannot be taken
for granted. The various interactions between the online viewers, museum
visitors, and objects in the museum reveal the digital screen's lack of boundaries, with the tacit understanding that the world on the "other side" of the
screen may also directly impact the world in which the viewer is situated.
Surveillance and control emerge as the flip side of the expansive spatial
realms associated with the Internet. If the virtual window analogy might fail
to capture this changed dynamic, what metaphor might be more appropriate? Lev Manovich argues that the computer screen constitutes a "battle-
field for incompatible definitions": it concurrently suggests both depth *and*
surface, opaqueness *and* transparency; it proposes the "image as illusionary
space *and* image as instrument for action."[19] His assessment is instructive

Telegarden Block Diagram

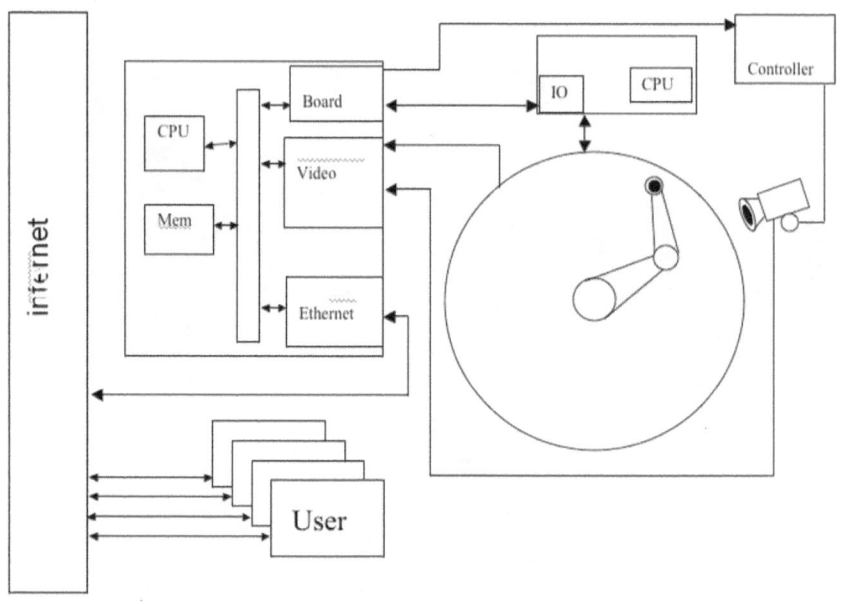

Ken Goldberg, *The Telegarden*, 1995–2004. Artist's diagram of
the complex interrelationship between the installation's various screen-based spaces and sites. Courtesy of Ken Goldberg.

in drawing out the computer screen's uneasy balancing act between screen-as-window and screen-as-flat-surface. However, it is the digital screen's capacity to serve as a connecting portal between multiple remote spatial environments, and not merely its ambivalent objecthood, that restructures the possibilities of media art spectatorship. The remarkable form of screen-reliant direct causality exhibited in Hershman's and Goldberg's computer-based installations is one heretofore unrealized in media art.

For these reasons, I propose that the appropriate allegory for the digital media screen is not a virtual window but an automatic sliding glass door: a pervasive yet unobtrusive object with exceptionally tenuous boundaries. Much like the commonplace automatic glass doors at an airport or super-market, any activity can inadvertently open or close the screen's connectivity, and there exists a certain ambiguity as to which side of the door/screen has instigated the action. As architectural theorist and historian Anthony Vidler succinctly puts it, the digital screen "[is] not a picture, and certainly not a surrogate window, but rather an ambiguous and unfixed location for a subject."[20] The viewing subject's inability to establish hierarchical relationships among potential arenas for the viewer's presence and action, as Vidler points out, can be intensely unsettling. Indeed, the computer screen facilitates open-ended and nearly limitless interactions between the spaces inside and beyond the screen and the viewer's own, ostensibly discrete psychological and phenomenal space.

Like Vidler, feminist theorist Elizabeth Grosz has approached this issue from the perspective of lived, architectural space. Her questions about the interimplication of screen spaces are provocative for thinking about the distinctive features of computer screen-reliant art spectatorship. She asks: "Can the computer screen act as the clear-cut barrier separating cyberspace from real space, the space of mental inhabitation from the physical space of corporeality? What if the boundary is more permeable than the smooth glassy finality of the screen?"[21] Even as Grosz's comments largely reinforce the pertinence of the automatic glass door metaphor, they also encourage us to make an important qualification: while the computer screen as automatic glass door offers a compelling way to think about this changed spatial dynamic, it can go only so far. After all, it provides a conceptual, not literal, parallel for thinking about screen-based spectatorship: there is no direct *body-to-body* contact between the screen-connected realms in networked digital installations as the glass door analogy might suggest. This distinction is pivotal. Parsing the subjective effects of the spectator's potentially detached and disembodied viewing experiences with digital spaces will be the chief concern of the rest of this chapter.

Between You and Me

The critical literature on *The Telegarden,* in contrast to that on *The Difference Engine #3,* rarely describes firsthand, in-person experiences with the material objects in the installation—in this case, the museum-bound patch of earth. After all, for visitors to the Austrian museum, there is something more exhausting than exhilarating about sowing a seed with a computer-powered robot arm when the seeds, soil, and tools to get the job done are only a few feet in front of you. It is revelatory that the discourse surrounding *The Telegarden* is preoccupied with the question of the garden's "realness"—an area of inquiry that Goldberg identifies as "telepistemology." That is, how can one know whether one is tending a real garden or a convincing facsimile? The artist offers some advice on the matter on the project's Web site: "What you are looking at is a live image of the Telegarden. . . .

If you are still not convinced that you are actually controlling a robot, click on the button to see the robot from a different perspective." Even the most generous visitor is likely to be unnerved by the seeming capriciousness of the qualification that follows, however: "[The robot] may be in your current position," or, Goldberg discloses, "It may be servicing someone else." Fair enough. The technological details involved in pulling off this project are complex and one could certainly envision how delays might happen. But how would one ever know for sure? Does it even matter?

As Gilles Deleuze first articulated in *Difference and Repetition*, there is an evocative way to understand this dynamic by radically undoing conventional distinctions between the "virtual" and the "real."[22] For Deleuze, all distinctions (mind and body, active and passive, actual and virtual) are collapsed or flattened into an even consistency on the plane of immanence. As a consequence, there are no preexisting hierarchies between the real and its representation; screen world(s) and the material world are coextensive (and thus equally "real") because both are images on the same plane of immanence.[23] Instead of troubling the question of whether Hershman's digitized museum or Goldberg's telegarden are "real," Deleuze, by proposing that no fixed hierarchies exist among such sites or experiences, presents a constructive way to rethink the proposition entirely. As helpful as this model is toward conceptualizing the ambiguous relationships among screen-reliant spaces and their connective interfaces, it unfortunately sidesteps the complexity of lived bodily experience that is central to media installation art and its spectatorship.

Ultimately, disembodiment and impassiveness toward screen-based spaces may be the threats posed by the preponderance of screen-mediated activity in our digital era. This can be conceived as an ethical issue. Philosopher Herbert Dreyfus writes: "Now, as more and more of our perception becomes indirect, read off various sorts of distance sensors and then presented by means of various sorts of displays, we are coming to realize how much of our knowledge is based on inferences that go beyond the evidence displayed on our screens."[24] The difficulty, as Dreyfus sees it, lies in how we respond to the growing variety of tele-experiences. He cautions that Cartesian skepticism becomes increasingly reasonable to the extent that "the reality mediated by this teletechnology can always be called into question."[25] Philosopher Michael Heim similarly underscores the risk of knowing the external world primarily through representations on screens. He likens contemporary screen-based communication to Leibniz's theory of monadism, in which monads themselves are the only things in the phenomenal world and everything else is simulations and representations. Heim's description of monadology is presented as a thinly veiled cautionary tale for a society awash in media screens: "Monads have no windows, but they do have terminals. The mental life of the monad—and the monad has no other life—is a procession of internal representations. ... [The monad] only knows what can be pictured."[26]

Both scholars point to the way in which the uncertain spatial dynamics engendered by telepresence and teleaction, whether in art environments or in everyday life, may lead spectators to doubt external reality—indeed, to question whether anything exists in the experiential material world outside of the world represented on the computer screen. Heim and Dreyfus suggest (the former implicitly and the latter explicitly) that these epistemological questions will be discredited only if viewing subjects have a sense of being in direct touch with real objects and people through the screen interface. Even to the degree that installations such as *The Difference Engine #3* and *The Telegarden* can persuasively establish a direct relationship between remote sites and viewers, however, it is perhaps even more significant that they productively reveal the extent to which certain foundational elements required for meaningful human-to-human communication remain glaringly absent from telepresence and teleaction. Consciously or otherwise, these artworks demonstrate that mere connectivity may not be enough to turn telepresence into presence.

Focusing specifically on the spatial aspects of technologically mediated experiences, philosopher Albert Borgmann identifies qualitative differences between what he terms proximal space and mediated space. He contrasts the suppleness of the former with the fragility of the latter and theorizes how only proximal space—face-to-face, body-to-body interaction—allows for continuity and repleteness.[27] This positive valuation of direct bodily experience echoes the proposition shared by phenomenology and feminist philosophy, which holds that subjects primarily learn to trust and feel intimacy via human touch and in the physical presence of other bodies. By now, the relevance for screen-based artistic production should be clear. If contemporary vision and communication are mediated more and more by digital screen-based technologies—if, that is, digital screens and their extensive yet unstable spatial realms orchestrate ever more interactions between subjects in art as in everyday life—then bodily contact between subjects and human interdependence risk becoming, on some level, conscious acts of will.[28]

Extending this critique to its logical conclusion, it is not enough merely to identify these new spatial realms. Critics and practitioners of new media art will need to develop an account of viewership appropriate for the spectator's unprecedented power to instantly control material reality from a distance through its screen-based image while also confronting the ways in which new viewing technologies can generate intensely destabilizing spatial dynamics for viewing subjects. The digital installations by Hershman and Goldberg underscore the curious condition that viewers may never really know if an environment represented on a screen is an actual remote locale or not, *even when it is.* Perhaps even more important, they persuasively demonstrate the ways in which activities represented in screen-based sites can easily fuse with material reality in terms of surveillance, control, and the teleactive and telepresent passage of subjects, objects, images, and information.

As further digital screen interfaces appear daily, installations like *The Difference Engine #3* and *The Telegarden* provide exceptional opportunities for critically evaluating the impact of these viewing technologies. Familiar art historical questions about real and illusionary spaces achieve a new urgency: What is our subjective relationship to these screen-reliant spaces? How does the subject's radically decentered and deterritorialized condition of being "neither here nor there" in relationship to a definitive scopic center ultimately challenge key premises of spectatorship as it has been conceived conventionally in art, film, and media theory? While these questions may preoccupy mainly new media theorists at present, they promise to be central concerns for screen-reliant artistic production in our digital age.

Thinking through Screens

"The limits of my language are the limits of my world," Wittgenstein once wrote. In *The Virtual Window,* Anne Friedberg adds new life to the philosopher's celebrated axiom by mapping it onto the visual register: "The limits and multiplicities of our frames of vision determine the boundaries and multiplicities of our world."[1] If this is so, and indeed this is a foundational premise of the present study, then it is incumbent on us as critics, historians, and practitioners to theorize and construct our interactions with screens (among our principal "frames of vision") as conscientiously as possible. This is the shared ambition of both *Screens: Viewing Media Installation Art* and the exemplary screen-reliant works of art that it has explored.

This book has provided a historical and critical context for the rise of gallery-based installations made with cinematic and electronic technologies, outlining their distinctive features and their particular relevance in terms of art history and spectatorship. By carefully assessing the operative conditions of what I call screen-reliant art spectatorship—attending to the complex ways in which screens orchestrate viewing postures, shift time and space, and separate subjects physically even as they connect them functionally—*Screens* introduced a theoretical model for critically assessing the moving-image installations that continue to proliferate since their inception in the mid-1960s. Situating present-day artistic production in relation to an over forty-year history allowed us to recognize that the issues and challenges posed by screen-based art are in fact not as new as certain "new media" scholars propose, even while providing a way to discern key characteristics, such as telepresence and teleaction, that do indeed constitute unprecedented modes of screen-reliant activity.

In contradistinction to many contemporary critical texts, *Screens* does not presuppose that artists should avoid employing advanced imaging and projection technologies or otherwise aspire to escape new media culture. Critical activity in what we might call our society of the screen requires a more nuanced approach. After all, as Margaret Morse correctly surmises, "aesthetic resistance depends on an older disposition of the subject in relation to the spectacle of an imaginary world framed and discrete behind the glass."[2] The art installations examined in this book are noteworthy precisely because they illuminate such transitions in models of spectatorship; these works explicitly engage dominant technologies of vision and underline the modes of mediation—material, psychic, ideological, and institutional—that are structural to interactions between viewers and screens. As I have argued throughout, a media art practice and criticism that is cognizant of the interimplicated relationship between screen objects, screen spaces, and viewing bodies is better prepared to confront the challenges (artistic, ethical, or otherwise) of the shifting connections among them.

Ultimately, the critical gesture of the media installations examined here is to call attention to the nature of screen-mediated visuality and to creatively disrupt our conventional relationships to media and imaging technologies in the process, however briefly. These works place the viewer–participant into an embodied circuit with a range of screen-reliant spatial and temporal realms and thus catalyze an awakening of their audiences to the materiality of the interface and the mediation inherent in vision and communication structured by screens. At the same time, however, our daily interactions with commercial and mass media screens of all kinds deeply inform screen-reliant spectatorship within the institutional context of the visual arts. Indeed, the production, reception, and exhibition of artworks made with film, video, and computer screens tend to reflect concurrent changes in mainstream media technologies.

Walter Benjamin's famous "The Work of Art in the Age of Mechanical Reproduction" serves as a useful model here, although perhaps in an unexpected way.[3] In evaluating early drafts of the Frankfurt School theorist's seminal text, film scholar Miriam Hansen explicates how Benjamin was able to imagine that the cinema constituted a "sensory-reflexive horizon in which the liberating as well as pathological effects of techno modernity" could be "articulated and engaged." Although this specific argument would be effectively edited out in subsequent iterations of the piece, Benjamin's initial conception of the cinema and cinematic reception as a site for critically disruptive "play" should not be overlooked. It is Hansen's effort to extend the implications of Benjamin's position to the current day, however, which proves especially inspiring in the current context. While she concedes that Benjamin's concept of " 'huge gain in room-for-play' " brought into being by the photographic media is, in her words, "more than matched by the industrial production and circulation of phantasmagoria," she intrepidly concludes with the following manifesto: "All the more reason for us, as historians, critics, and theorists, artists, writers, and teachers, to take Benjamin's gamble with cinema seriously and to wage an aesthetics of play, understood as a political ecology of the senses, on a par with the most advanced technologies."[4] It is arguably by engaging in such an aesthetics of play that screen-reliant installations allow contemporary viewers the opportunity to reconceptualize their relationships with dominant technologies of visualization.

Much scholarly work remains to be done on the provocative issues surrounding media screens and art.[5] At the same time, issues of access and preservation pose considerable obstacles. Outside of contemporary exhibitions, it is difficult to observe many screen-reliant installations at all, much less to see them in their original configurations. This is due to multiple factors, including issues of site-specificity (which is, after all, a common dilemma for the majority of experiential and site-based artworks created since 1960) but also, and equally important, the problem of technological obsolescence. Media technologies are quickly outdated and media artworks are no exception; in many cases it proves impossible to operate or restore the technological apparatus, which, insofar as it served as a defining element of the viewer-screen interface, was once central to the artwork's very meaning. While scholars and institutions are working diligently to address issues of preservation and access for museum-based media art, many thorny issues over artistic intention, ephemerality, and the commodity status of individual works remain unresolved.[6] With limited opportunities for first-hand viewing of historic pieces, writing about this kind of artistic production requires patient review of archival materials, exhibition reviews, interviews, documentary photographs, and the like. Would-be audiences must also content themselves for the most part with (still) photographs documenting the initial installation of a given moving-image environment. The complexity of this type of research endeavor is clearly more than matched, however, by the foundational importance of these evocative works for theories of spectatorship in art history and film and media studies.

At present, as viewers are routinely constructed as screen subjects, in art as in everyday life, the urgency to appreciate the complex interactions between bodies and media screens is unmistakable. Contemporary visuality is so overwhelmingly defined by screens—from cell phones and laptops to Jumbotrons and electronic billboards—that the dramatic subjective effects of screen-based viewing often go unnoticed. Art historian Jonathan Crary articulated the perils of ignoring these developments in relationship to contemporary digital culture as early as 1984, pointing out how "the screens of home computer and word processor have succeeded the automobile as the 'core products' in an on-going relocation and hierarchization of production processes."[7] Even as he carefully enunciates the disciplinary aspects of digital technologies, however, it is precisely at the body-screen interface—"in the immediate vicinity of the terminal screen"—that he glimpses a prospective criticality: "We must recognize the fundamental incapacity of capitalism ever to rationalize the circuit between body and computer," Crary argues, "and realize that this circuit is the site of a latent but potentially volatile disequilibrium."[8] It is this very condition of disequilibrium that the installations examined in this book creatively exploit: by asking us to "think through" our thinking *through* media screens, these works of art immeasurably enrich our arena of contemporary cultural activity arbitrated by screens, both inside the art gallery and beyond.

Notes

Introduction

1. Vivian Sobchack, "The Scene of the Screen: Envisioning Cinematic and Electronic 'Presence,'" in *Film and Theory: An Anthology*, ed. Robert Stam and Toby Miller (London: Blackwell, 2000), 69.

2. Among the scholars who have scrutinized these issues from the perspective of film and media studies, Jean Baudrillard, Anne Friedberg, Erkki Huhtamo, Lev Manovich, Margaret Morse, Charles Musser, Sherry Turkle, Paul Virilio, and Siegfried Zielinski offer the most comprehensive accounts. Friedberg's approach in *The Virtual Window* is exemplary for the present study: "The everyday frames through which we see things—the 'material' frames of movie screens, television sets, computer screens, car windshields—provide compelling evidence of the dominance of the frame and its visual system. A study of the frame itself will tell us more than a study of the intrinsic and extrinsic meanings of what the frame contains." Anne Friedberg, *The Virtual Window: From Alberti to Microsoft* (Cambridge, Mass.: MIT Press), 14.

3. Other notable exhibitions in recent years that feature a plethora of screen-based artistic production include those of Catherine David, Raymond Bellour, et al., *Passages de l'image* (Paris: Centre Georges Pompidou, 1991); Jan Debbaut, Jean-Christophe Royoux, et al., *Cinéma Cinéma: Contemporary Art and the Cinematic Experience* (Eindhoven: Stedelijk Museum/NAi Publishers Rotterdam, 1999); Stan Douglas, Christopher Eamon, Joachim Jaeger, and Gabriele Knapstein, *Beyond Cinema: The Art of Projection* (Berlin: Hamburger Bahnhof, 2006); Antje Ehmann and Harun Farocki, *Kino wie noch nie/Cinema Like Never Before* (Vienna: Generali Foundation, 2006); and Marc Meyer, ed., *Being and Time: The Emergence of Video Projection* (Buffalo, N.Y.: Albright-Knox Art Gallery, 1996). While differences between gallery-based and museum-based spectatorship are not unimportant, this book focuses on the conditions that largely pertain to both settings.

4. The correspondences between the screen-based technologies created within commercial, entertainment, industrial, and military applications and those used in the visual arts since the 1960s are appreciable, of course, in both affirmative and oppositional

manifestations. For a recent analysis of the implicit "validation of the machinic presence" in projected-image installations and the relevance of this condition toward theorizations of the viewing subject, see Dominique Païni, "Should We Put an End to Projection?" *October* 110 (Fall 2004): 32. The terms of this critique in relationship to contemporary media art were prefigured in many ways by writings in the 1970s by Annette Michelson, Peter Wollen, and others. We will return to these important arguments in detail in chapter 4.

5. Stanley Cavell, *The World Viewed: Reflections on the Ontology of Film* (Cambridge, Mass.: Harvard University Press, 1971).

6. Critics remain divided over what to call this mode of art practice; other potential labels include "moving image," "multiscreen/multiprojection" or "projected image" installation, "the other cinema" (Raymond Bellour), and "the cinema of exhibition" (Jean-Christophe Royoux). My choice of the term "screen-reliant installation" is intended to cross medium-specific boundaries and draw attention to the structuring role of screens in media installation art spectatorship.

7. The foundational historical text for evaluating the relationship between new technologies, modernism, and art spectatorship is Jonathan Crary's extremely influential *Techniques of the Observer: On Vision and Modernity in the Nineteenth Century* (Cambridge, Mass.: MIT Press, 1990). See Erkki Huhtamo's "Elements of Screenology: Archaeology of the Screen" for a comprehensive historical overview of types of screens, *Iconics* 7 (2004): 31–82. One might even include other premodern art forms such as medieval stained glass or Roman wall painting as early examples of "screen-based" art viewing.

8. While it is important to recognize that the critical ambitions of installation art are not wholly unprecedented, and that critical reflexivity about the institutions of art and the museum does predate the 1960s (for instance, early-twentieth-century avant-garde Dada and surrealist exhibitions pioneered the concept of making the viewer conscious of the exhibition space, most notably the art and writing of Marcel Duchamp), fundamentally different notions of art, space, and the spectator—and a self-reflexive interest in the relationship between them—developed in the 1960s that break with past models.

9. As will be discussed in chapter 1, I use the term "screen-reliant" as opposed to "screen-based" to signal that a screen is a performative category and that "screen-mediated" viewing is in no way confined to conventional flat, rectangular surfaces.

10. While their specific critical investments vary, scholars such as Mieke Bal, John Berger, Norman Bryson, Jonathan Crary, James Elkins, Michael Fried, Griselda Pollock, and Jacqueline Rose have focused on questions of spectatorship and the gaze within the context of art history.

11. Judith Mayne, *Cinema and Spectatorship* (New York: Routledge, 1993), 32.

12. Key figures associated with apparatus and feminist psychoanalytic film theory include Jean-Louis Baudry, Christian Metz, Laura Mulvey, Mary Ann Doane, Joan Copjec, Constance Penley, and Theresa de Lauretis. Mayne offers an excellent summary of spectatorship theories and debates in her *Cinema and Spectatorship*.

13. Note that I employ the terms "spectator" and "viewer" advisedly. While the viewing subjects of media installations are simultaneously actors and observers, subjects and objects, there is no term perfectly suited to emphasizing this fluidity and contingency.

14. Film scholar and theorist Philip Rosen's clarification is helpful here: "If one investigates the apparatus by outlining the spectatorial ideals of a certain technology of representation—its aspirations, as it were, for the subject—this is not the same as finding an automatically and universally efficacious implementation of those ideals." Philip Rosen, ed. *Narrative, Apparatus, Ideology: Film Theory Reader* (New York: Columbia University Press, 1986), 283.

15. Apparatus theory has been critiqued for being complicit with its object of analysis and suggesting that film viewing inevitably reinforces a masterful masculinist viewing position. Similarly informed by psychoanalysis, feminist scholars have done much to refine apparatus-based theories by attending to the forms of identity and embodiment neglected by earlier theorists. Psychoanalytic models in turn have been critiqued for ignoring the historical specificity of viewers and visual production, failing to consider issues of class, ethnicity, race, sexuality, and other forms of difference, and even for misunderstanding psychoanalysis itself. See Mayne, *Cinema and Spectatorship*, and Rosen, *Narrative, Apparatus, Ideology*, 281–85, for a summary of these debates. For a cogent discussion of the challenges posed by what has been called transnational or cross-cultural spectatorship, for example, see Ella Habiba Shohat and Robert Stam, "Film Theory and Spectatorship in the Age of the 'Posts,'" in *Reinventing Film Studies*, ed. Christine Gledhill and Linda Williams (London and New York: Arnold, 2000).

16. Vivian Sobchack, *The Address of the Eye: Film and Phenomenology* (Princeton, N.J.: Princeton University Press, 1992), 14–15.

17. Mark B. N. Hansen, *New Philosophy for New Media* (Cambridge and London: MIT Press, 2004) and *Bodies in Code* (London: Routledge, 2006); Amelia Jones, *Self/Image: Technology, Representation, and the Contemporary Subject* (London: Routledge, 2006); Laura Marks, *Touch: Sensuous Theory and Multisensory Media* (Minneapolis: University of Minnesota Press, 2002); Vivian Sobchack, *Carnal Thoughts: Embodiment and Moving Image Culture* (Berkeley: University of California Press, 2004) and *The Address of the Eye;* and Kaja Silverman, *World Spectators* (Stanford, Calif.: Stanford University Press, 2000). Silverman's text is especially evocative in her careful development and expansion of Jacques Lacan's notion of the *écran* (screen).

18. Michael Archer, "Installation Art," in *Installation Art*, ed. Nicolas De Oliveira, Andrew Benjamin, Nicola Oxley, and Michael Petry (Washington, D.C.: Smithsonian Press, 1994); Claire Bishop, *Installation Art: A Critical History* (New York: Routledge, 2005); Rosalind Krauss, *A Voyage on the North Sea: Art in the Age of the Post-Medium Condition* (London: Thames and Hudson, 2000); Julie Reiss, *From Margin to Center: The Spaces of Installation Art* (Cambridge, Mass.: MIT Press, 2000); and Erika Suderburg, ed., *Space, Site, Intervention: Situating Installation Art* (Minneapolis: University of Minnesota Press, 2000). It is important to note that, although Krauss's *A Voyage on the North Sea* rigorously examines artworks contingent upon the viewer's experience with media screens of various kinds, she studiously refuses to consider them in relationship to what she disdainfully refers to as the "international fashion of installation and intermedia work" (56).

19. See, for example, George Baker, "Film beyond Its Limits," *Grey Room* 25 (2006); Raymond Bellour, "D'un autre cinema," *Trafic* 34 (2000): 5–21; Daniel Birnbaum, *Chronology* (New York: Lukas and Sternberg, 2005); Sabine Breitwieser, *White Cube/*

Black Box: Skulpturensammlung: Video Installation Film (exh. cat.) (Vienna: Generali Foundation, 1996); Eric De Bruyn, "Topological Pathways of Post-Minimalism," *Grey Room* 25 (2006); Douglas et al., *Beyond Cinema* (exh. cat.); Ursula Frohne, ed., *Video Cult/ures: Multimedial Installationen der 90er Jahre* (exh. cat.) (Karlsruhe and Cologne: ZKM, 1999); Jackie Hatfield, "Expanded Cinema and Narrative," *Millennium Film Journal* 39–40 (2003): 51–66; Chrissie Iles, ed., *Into the Light: The Projected Image in American Art, 1964–1977* (exh. cat.) (New York: Whitney Museum, 2001); Branden Joseph, "Plastic Empathy: The Ghost of Robert Whitman," *Grey Room* 25 (Fall 2006): 64–91; Tanya Leighton, ed., *Art and the Moving Image: A Critical Reader* (London: Tate Museum and Afterall Press, 2008); Janine Marchessault and Susan Lord, ed., *Fluid Screens/Expanded Cinema* (Toronto: University of Toronto Press, 2007); Matthias Michalka, ed., *X-Screen: Film Installation and Actions in the 1960s and 1970s (exh. cat.) (Koln: Verlag der Buchhandlung Walther Konig, 2003);* Malcolm Turvey et al., "Roundtable: The Projected Image in Contemporary Art," *October* 104 (Spring 2003): 71–96; Jean-Christophe Royoux, "Cinema as Exhibition, Duration as Space," *ArtPress* 262 (November 2000): 36–41; and Jonathan Walley, "The Material of Film and the Idea of Cinema: Contrasting Practices in Sixties and Seventies Avant-Garde Film," *October* 103 (2003): 15–30. Early investigations include Anne-Marie Duguet, "Dispositifs," *Communications* 48 (1988): 221–42; Martin Friedman, ed., *Projected Images* (exh. cat.) (Minneapolis: Walker Art Center, 1974); Doug Hall and Sally Jo Fifer, ed., *Illuminating Video* (New York: Aperture/Bay Area Video Coalition, 1991); John Hanhardt, "The Passion for Perceiving: Expanded Forms of Film and Video Art," *Art Journal* (Fall 1985): 213–16; Birgit Hein and Wulf Herzogenrath, ed., *Film as Film: Formal Experiment in Film 1910–1975* (exh. cat.) (London: Arts Council of Great Britain, 1979); Dorine Mignot, ed., *The Luminous Image* (exh. cat.) (Amsterdam: Stedelijk Museum, 1984); and Gene Youngblood, *Expanded Cinema* (New York: E. P. Dutton and Co., 1970). Among these, Birnbaum's *Chronology* is the most sustained and rigorous book-length inquiry into the topic of media installation and its spectatorship to date.

20. Recent art historical investigations on the question of the "post-medium" condition are promising in this respect, if somewhat unsatisfying. Rosalind Krauss proposes the term "technical support" as a way to avoid the unwanted positivism of the term "medium" (which she contends has been reductively associated with the specific physical, material support of a traditional artistic genre). See Rosalind Krauss, "Two Moments from the Post-Medium Condition," *October* 116 (Spring 2006): 55–62; *A Voyage on the North Sea;* and " 'And Then Turn Away?' An Essay on James Coleman," *October* 81 (1997): 5–33. Also note that the term medium-specific (or media-specific) varies greatly across different disciplines; the objections I make to the use of medium-specific criteria for analyzing media installation art are related to the legacy of Greenbergian formalist modernism and do not apply to the way the term is used, for example, in literary and cultural studies.

21. Turvey et al., "Roundtable," 71–96.

22. On the issue of convergence see especially Kay Hoffmann and Thomas Elsaesser, ed., *Cinema Futures: Cain, Abel, or Cable: The Screen Arts in the Digital Age, Film Culture in Transition* (Amsterdam: Amsterdam University Press, 1998), and Henry Jenkins, *Convergence Culture* (New York: New York University Press, 2006).

23. As this book goes to press, the organizational rubric of "screen studies" has become commonplace in film and media studies. See, for example, Annette Kuhn, ed., "Screen Theorizing Today," *Screen* (Spring 2009), which assesses the state of the field of "screen studies" and our contemporary "screenscape." While not self-identified as "screen studies" per se, other representative examples (in addition to those already listed in note 2) might include Jay David Bolter and Diane Gromola, *Windows and Mirrors* (Cambridge, Mass.: MIT Press, 2003), and Michele White, *The Body and the Screen: Theories of Internet Spectatorship* (Cambridge, Mass.: MIT Press, 2006). However, these strictly new media studies do not address the relevance of the viewer-screen interface for *art* spectatorship in particular. Anna McCarthy's *Ambient Television: Visual Culture and Public Space* (Durham, N.C.: Duke University Press, 2001) and Margaret Morse's *Virtualities: Television, Media Art, and Cyberculture* (Bloomington: Indiana University Press, 1998) offer compelling studies of video's spatial relationships and its material culture, although both focus primarily on commercial television screens in non-art public settings. For an art historical inquiry explicitly concerned with "screens," see Haim Finkelstein, *The Screen in Surrealist Art and Thought* (London: Ashgate Press, 2007).

24. Lev Manovich, *The Language of New Media* (Cambridge, Mass.: MIT Press, 2001); Huhtamo, "Elements of Screenology," 31–82. Approaching the topic from the point of view of architectural history and theory, Giuliana Bruno argues in her *Public Intimacy: Architecture and the Visual Arts* that a "screen of vital cultural memory" has come to shape our contemporary visual culture (Cambridge, Mass.: MIT Press, 2007).

1. Interface Matters

1. Michael Fried, "Art and Objecthood," *Artforum* (Summer 1967): 23 n. 16. For a recent historical evaluation of this essay in relationship to art and technology in the 1960s see Pamela Lee, *Chronophobia: On Time in the Art of the 1960s* (Cambridge, Mass.: MIT Press, 2004), especially chapter 1, "Presentness Is Grace."

2. Of course, media screens have not always functioned exclusively or even primarily as thresholds onto virtual worlds. Tom Gunning's classic study "The Cinema of Attractions: Early Cinema, Its Spectator, and the Avant-Garde," for example, suggests how early cinema (pre-1906) enjoyed a different relation to its spectator, emphasizing the exhibitionist, vaudevillelike "cinema of attractions" that accentuated the new cinema technology itself. In *Early Cinema: Space, Frame, Narrative,* ed. Thomas Elsaesser and Adam Barker (London: British Film Institute, 1990). Dominique Païni speculates that expanded cinema projects in the 1960s may in fact come closer to approximating the origins of cinema than classical Hollywood film for this reason. Païni, "Should We Put an End to Projection?", 31.

3. The screen is an extremely ambivalent material object, functioning simultaneously as a material surface and as an immaterial or conceptual threshold to imagery or other information. I have written about the screen's ambiguous hybrid status elsewhere. See Kate Mondloch, "Not Just a Window: Reflections on the Media Screen," *Vectors: Journal of Culture and Technology in a Dynamic Vernacular* (Spring 2006): np. Deleuze observes that "everything" can be a screen in *Cinema 2: The Time-Image,*

although he leaves undeveloped the subjective consequences that these "virtual windows" generate as material objects. Gilles Deleuze, *Cinema 2*, trans. Hugh Tomlinson and Robert Galeta (Minneapolis: University of Minnesota Press, 1989), 215.

4. This is famously articulated by Hal Foster in "The Crux of Minimalism," in *The Return of the Real* (Cambridge, Mass.: MIT Press, 1996). As I demonstrate in chapter 4, the phenomenological and anti-illusionist interpretation of postminimalist North American media art production is well established; Benjamin Buchloh, Regina Cornwell, Rosalind Krauss, Annette Michelson, and Peter Wollen, although primarily concerned with film as opposed to other media arts, initiated the important project of charting the intersections between advanced art and film practices in a series of articles in the 1970s in journals such as *Artforum, Film Culture, Interfunktionen,* and *Studio International.*

5. Critic and artist Brian O'Doherty notably identified a shift in art spectatorship associated with the turn toward "context as content" as early as 1976. See Brian O'Doherty, *Inside the White Cube: The Ideology of the Gallery Space* (Santa Monica, Calif.: Lapis Press, 1986).

6. Developed within the context of film studies in the 1970s, this theory is concerned with defining how cinema works as an "institutional apparatus" consisting of a programmed relationship between the film, the film projector, the screen, and the spectator. As described by film theorist Christian Metz in 1975 in his seminal essay "The Imaginary Signifier" (English trans. 1982): "The cinematic institution is not just the cinema industry... it is also the mental machinery—another industry—which spectators 'accustomed to the cinema' have internalized historically and which has adapted them to the consumption of films.... The institution is outside us and inside us, indistinctly collective and intimate, sociological and psychoanalytic." Christian Metz, "The Imaginary Signifier: Psychoanalysis and the Cinema," in *The Imaginary Signifier: Psychoanalysis and the Cinema,* trans. Celia Britton, Annwyl Williams, and Ben Brewster (Bloomington: Indiana University Press, 1982), 7. In addition to Metz's essay, key texts on apparatus theory include Jean Louis Baudry, "Ideological Effects of the Basic Cinematographic Apparatus," *Cinéthique* 7–8 (1970), and "The Apparatus: Metapsychological Approaches to the Impression of Reality in Cinema," *Communications* 23 (1975). Both essays are reprinted in translation in Rosen, *Narrative, Apparatus, Ideology,* 286–98 and 299–318.

7. Psychoanalytic theory, especially Lacan's theorization of the mirror stage, was at the forefront of these debates. Jacques Lacan, "The Mirror Stage as Formative of the Function of the I as Revealed in Psychoanalytic Experience," in *Écrits: A Selection,* trans. Alan Sheridan (London: Tavistock, and New York: Norton, 1975).

8. See Baudry, "Ideological Effects of the Basic Cinematographic Apparatus." Baudry refines this line of critique in his more psychoanalytically informed 1975 essay "The Apparatus: Metapsychological Approaches to the Impression of Reality in Cinema." Both essays are reprinted in Rosen, *Narrative, Apparatus, Ideology,* 286–318.

9. The New Museum of Contemporary Art's *From Receiver to Remote Control: The TV Set* (1990), a little-known exhibition crated by Matthew Geller that prominently displayed television sets/screens *as objects* in the museum space, constitutes a noteworthy exception within an art gallery setting.

10. See, for example, Fredric Jameson, *Postmodernism, or the Cultural Logic of Late Capitalism* (Durham, N.C.: Duke University Press, 1990), especially chapter 3, "Video: Surrealism without the Unconscious," and Paul Virilio, *The Vision Machine* (London: British Film Institute, 1994).

11. Media scholar Anna McCarthy argues for what she calls a site-specific understanding of television in "From Screen to Site: Television's Material Culture and Its Place," *October* 98 (Fall 2001): 93–111. See also McCarthy, *Ambient Television: Visual Culture and Public Space* (Durham, N.C.: Duke University Press, 2001), for a detailed analysis of the physical placement of television sets outside of the domestic realm and the corresponding implications for televisual spectatorship.

12. Media ecology offers a useful model here. As Matthew Fuller observes in *Media Ecologies: Materialist Energies in Art and Technoculture* (Cambridge, Mass.: MIT Press, 2005), "Complex objects such as media systems—understood here as processes, or elements in a composition as much as 'things'—have become informational as much as physical, but *without losing any of their fundamental materiality*" (emphasis added). The concept of a media ecology in relationship to media art originated with Gregory Bateson within the context of the activist publication *Radical Software*. See also David Joselit, *Feedback: Television against Democracy* (Cambridge, Mass.: MIT Press, 2007), and William Kaizen, "Steps to an Ecology of Communication: *Radical Software,* Dan Graham, and the Legacy of Gregory Bateson," *Art Journal* 67, no. 3 (2008): 86–107.

13. Paul Sharits, "Statement Regarding Multiple Screen/Sound 'Locational' Film Environments—Installations," *Film Culture* 65–66 (1978): 79–80. (Sharits contends that he first wrote this in 1974, hence the date cited in the text.)

14. Rosalind Krauss, "Paul Sharits," in *Paul Sharits: Dream Displacement and Other Projects,* ed. Linda Cathcart (New York: Albright-Knox Art Gallery, 1976), np; reprinted in *Film Culture* 65–66 (1978): 92. Federico Windhausen offers a historical reading of Sharits's shifting interest in spectator participation in his "Paul Sharits and the Active Spectator," in *Art and the Moving Image: A Critical Reader,* ed. Tanya Leighton (London: Tate Publishing, 2008), 122–39.

15. Celebrated American film critic P. Adams Sitney first coined the term "structural film" in 1969 to describe a new tendency in North American experimental filmmaking exemplified by the works of Sharits, Snow, Tony Conrad, George Landow, Ernie Gear, Hollis Frampton, and Joyce Wieland. Applying a strict formalist criticism, Sitney contended that their films constituted "cinematic propositions in a rigorously ordered form." "The *shape* of the whole film is predetermined and simplified," Sitney argued, "and it is that shape that is the primal impression of the film. . . . What content it has is minimal and subsidiary to the outline." In spite of the name Sitney coined to describe it, North American "structural film" has nothing to do with structuralism as a philosophy; he apparently chose the label to denote the way in which the work's "structure" is determined in advance. P. Adams Sitney, "Structural Film," *Film Culture* 47 (Summer 1969); reprinted in P. Adams Sitney, "Structural Film," in *Film Culture Reader* (New York: Praeger Publishers, 1970), 327. Annette Michelson distinguished related developments as early as 1966 when she observed that "these films, in their intransigent autonomy, make an almost wholly plastic use of reference and allusion, by no means excluding extra plastic resonances, but animated by a sense of structure as

progress-in-time so absolute and compelling that very little else has room or time enough in which to 'happen.'" ("Film and the Radical Aspiration," reprinted in Sitney's *Film Culture Reader,* 419.) Foreshadowing the confusion to come in regard to descriptive terms for film art, Sitney's coda to the 1970 printing of his essay includes reference to the "distinguished sculptors" (he mentions Richard Serra, Bruce Nauman, Robert Morris, and Hollis Frampton) currently developing a sort of film art practice that Sitney confirmed could not be adequately understood within the framework of structural film (346). See also Sitney, *Visionary Film: The American Avant-Garde* (New York: Oxford University Press, 1974).

16. Sharits, "Statement Regarding Multiple Screen/Sound 'Locational' Film Environments—Installations," 79–80.

17. These are known as "flicker films" because they depict short bursts or "flickers" of barely comprehensible optical information lasting from a single frame (1/24th of a second, slightly below visibility) to a sequence twelve frames long. Peter Kubelka, Tony Conrad, Takahiko Iimura, Fred Drummond, and Birgit and Wilhelm Hein are among the filmmakers first associated with the flicker film genre.

18. Paul Sharits, "Notes on Films," *Film Culture* 47 (Summer 1969): 14.

19. Sitney, "Structural Film," in *Film Culture Reader,* 326–48. For a recent historical account of structural film (including so-called "flicker films") within the context of expanded art and media experimentation in the 1960s and 1970s, see Branden Joseph, *Beyond the Dream Syndicate: Tony Conrad and the Arts after Cage* (Cambridge, Mass.: Zone Books, 2008), especially chapter 6, "The Flicker."

20. Sharits's comments regarding the final section of *T,O,U,C,H,I,N,G* indicate his shift from predominantly formal to more phenomenological concerns: "I wanted to visualize 'inverse pain' as a kind of imploding reverberation of the picture edge—the screen appears to collapse, in rhythmic pulses, into itself. This latter mode—of introducing shapes into the frame which were reflective of the film frame's perimeter-shape and which acted as a commentary on the state of consciousness of the film's protagonist at that point in the (backwards) 'narrative'—struck me later as being somewhat too related to strategies of painting, as did other aspects of my films of that early period." Paul Sharits, "Hearing: Seeing," *Film Culture* 65–66 (1978): 72.

21. Paul Sharits, "Exhibition/Frozen Frames: Regarding the 'Frozen Film Frame' Series—A Statement for the '5th International Experimental Film Festival,'" *Film Culture* 65–66 (1978): 82.

22. There are many more discoveries for the viewer related to the film's material process that I cannot thoroughly explore in the body of the text. For instance, in studying the film imagery, viewers quickly notice the exposed sprocket holes that seem to indicate the filmstrip has slipped off the tracks of the projector. (Sprocket holes are the parallel lines of holes that run the length of the celluloid and secure the film as it runs through the projector.) On closer inspection, it is clear that the sprocket "holes" are recorded images that are revealed when scratched lines occasionally pass over the supposed holes at the top of the strip. (The scratched lines on each film were created over two generations of recording and projecting. Sharits scratched the emulsion of each filmstrip, back-projected it onto a screen, rephotographed this off of the screen, and scratched the new image.) Thus, the scratches from the "original" film appear as blurred bands of light (images of scratches) that contrast with the sharply defined scratched

lines on the current film's surface ("real" scratches that developed over the course of the art exhibition). Sharits explained: "The sprocket holes that were really empty spaces now are images. Even though they're passing white light, they're acting as images, as things." "Paul Sharits Interview with Linda Cathcart," *Paul Sharits: Dream Displacement and Other Projects,* np.

23. That said, it is important to acknowledge the experimental films that occupy a halfway point between these two models. In addition to so-called structural filmmakers, film artists such as Bruce Conner, Carolee Schneemann, and Stan Brakhage have created films whose subject matter or narrative focuses on the materiality of the medium and/or the apparatus, even while the works themselves are meant to be experienced in conventional theatrical/cinematic viewing conditions. I have discussed this discrepancy at length elsewhere. See Kate Mondloch, "The Matter of Illusionism," in *Screen/Space,* ed. Tamara Trodd and Samantha Lackey (Manchester, UK: University of Manchester Press, forthcoming). For a historical investigation of the "paracinematic" in work by artists such as Paul Sharits, Anthony McCall, and Tony Conrad, which privileges the conceptual over the material, see Jonathan Walley, "The Material of Film and the Idea of Cinema: Contrasting Practices in Sixties and Seventies Avant-Garde Film," *October* 103 (2003): 15–30.

24. John Rajchman, "Deleuze's Time, or How the Cinematic Image Changes Our Idea of Art," in *Art and the Moving Image,* ed. Leighton, 326. On the specific relevance of the screen for Deleuze, Rajchman suggestively explains: "We see that from the start there is a sense in which the screen was less an illusionist window or ersatz classical stage than a moving frame with an 'out-of-frame' that allows movement and time to be rendered in new ways that would move beyond the conceptions of space in classical painting or theater, *suggesting alternatives to them*" (320). Emphasis added.

25. Nicole Gingras, "Michael Snow: Transparency and Light," trans. Frank Straschitz, *Art Press* 234 (April 1998): 23.

26. *Artforum* X, no. 1 (September 1971): 63.

27. Regina Cornwell, "Michael Snow," in Martin Friedman et al., *Projected Images: Peter Campus, Rockne Krebs, Paul Sharits, Michael Snow, Ted Victoria, Robert Whitman* (Minneapolis: Walker Art Center, 1974), 26, 31. Cornwell's 1978 comments on Snow's oeuvre in *Film Reader* are apposite; the critic noted that his film-based works share with minimalism a "concern with the object, immediate presence, holistic and dehierarchized structure, and distancing." Unlike minimal art, however, Snow's pieces deliberately and unapologetically retain "a representational image." Although written specifically in regard to the artist's experimental film *Wavelength,* this powerful observation applies broadly to Snow's media installations as well. Regina Cornwell, "Hitting on 'A Lot of Near Mrs.,'" *Film Reader* 3 (1978): 241.

28. Media installation's early critical reception is explored in more detail in chapter 4.

29. Païni, "Should We Put an End to Projection?" 44.

30. Snow's own remarks would appear to substantiate this interpretation. In correspondence with art critic and historian Thierry de Duve, Snow writes: "I do think that my work 'is more radical than that,' and why I think that is related to my attempt to make the work a 'now,' 'materialist,' yes a 'modernist' experience as well as to have and to direct the references elsewhere of representation, 'away' and back to you and the work itself." Michael Snow, "A Letter to Thierry de Duve," *Parachute* 78 (1995): 63.

31. Cited in Cornwell, "Michael Snow," in Friedman et al., *Projected Images*, 30.

32. It is worth noting that the critical reception of all of Snow's film and video work between 1966 (the year Snow created his celebrated film *Wavelength*) and 1975 is largely circumscribed by the critical discourse surrounding structural-materialist film as defined by the two most influential critics associated with British experimental film, Malcolm Le Grice and Peter Gidal—both of whom were primarily associated with the pivotal London Filmmakers' Co-op that Le Grice established in the late 1960s. Key texts include Peter Gidal, "Theory and Definition of Structural/Materialist Film," *Studio International* 189/190 (December 1975): 189–96, and Malcolm Le Grice, *Abstract Film and Beyond* (Cambridge, Mass.: MIT Press, 1977). For a useful analysis of the consequences of the curious (mis)reception of Snow's film-based oeuvre in the 1960s and 1970s, see Bart Testa, "An Axiomatic Cinema: Michael Snow's Films," in *The Michael Snow Project: Presence and Absence: The Film of Michael Snow 1956–1991*, ed. Jim Shedder (Toronto: Art Gallery of Ontario/Knopf, 1995).

33. The shot/reverse-shot editing technique shows a single character looking (often offscreen) at another character, immediately followed by the second character looking "back" at the first. The spectator automatically and somewhat irrationally assumes that the viewers are looking at each other because the characters are shown facing different directions. On the topic of cinematic suture in film studies, see especially Jean-Pierre Oudart, "Cinema and Suture," *Screen* 18 (1977), and Stephen Heath, "Narrative Space," *Screen* 3 (Fall 1976), as well as Kaja Silverman's helpful analysis of suture theory in her *The Subject of Semiotics* (New York: Oxford University Press, 1983).

34. Roland Barthes, "Leaving the Movie Theater," in *The Rustle of Language* (Berkeley and Los Angeles: University of California Press, 1989), 348.

35. Vivian Sobchack, among others, has written extensively on the phenomenology of viewing moving images within the institutional context of the cinema. See her *Address of the Eye: A Phenomenology of Film Experience* (Princeton, N.J.: Princeton University Press, 1992) and *Carnal Thoughts: Embodiment and Moving Image Culture* (Berkeley: University of California Press, 2004). It is interesting to note that neuroscientific studies over the past few decades would appear to confirm that embodiment is inseparable from the cognitive activity of the brain; in other words, all viewing is *inherently* embodied viewing, making it impossible to fully distinguish between activity in the feeling body and in the brain. See, for example, Joseph Ledoux, *The Emotional Brain: The Emotional Underpinnings of Emotional Life* (New York: Simon and Schuster, 1996), as well as Antonio R. Damasio, *Descartes' Error: Emotion, Reason, and the Human Brain* (New York: G. P. Putnam, 1994); *The Feeling of What Happens: Body and Emotion in the Making of Consciousness* (New York: Harcourt Brace, 1999); and *Looking for Spinoza: Joy, Sorrow, and the Feeling Brain* (Orlando, Fla.: Harcourt Brace, 2003).

2. Body and Screen

1. Media scholars such as E. Ann Kaplan and John Ellis have argued that television technology and its characteristic forms of flow produce a spectatorship qualitatively different from that of cinema (Ellis specifically articulates this difference in terms of the gaze and the glance). John Ellis, *Visible Fictions* (London: Routledge and Kegan Paul,

1982), 138. E. Ann Kaplan, *Rocking around the Clock: Music Television, Post Modernism, and Consumer Culture* (New York: Routledge, 1987). For a contrasting, intermedial approach to the conditions of specifically electronic media spectatorship, see Jeffrey Sconce, *Haunted Media: Electronic Presence from Telegraphy to Television* (Durham, N.C.: Duke University Press, 2000).

2. Christof Koch, *The Quest for Consciousness: A Neurobiological Approach* (Englewood, Colo.: Roberts and Company Publishers, 2004), 161.

3. The critical thinkers associated with the Frankfurt School were the first to theorize the relationship between advanced technologies and the "culture industry." See Max Horkheimer and Theodor Adorno, *Dialectic of Enlightenment,* trans. John Cumming (New York: Seabury, 1972). Benjamin Buchloh is among the foremost proponents of these ideas in the realm of contemporary art history and criticism. See his *Neo-Avantgarde and Culture Industry: Essays on European and American Art from 1955 to 1975* (Cambridge, Mass.: MIT Press, 2000).

4. See, for example, Matthew Fuller, *Media Ecologies: Materialist Energies in Art and Technoculture* (Cambridge, Mass.: MIT Press, 2005); Alexander Galloway and Eugene Thacker, *The Exploit: A Theory of Networks* (Minneapolis: University of Minnesota Press, 2007); Joselit, *Feedback: Television against Democracy;* and Joseph, *Beyond the Dream Syndicate: Tony Conrad and the Arts after Cage.*

5. I borrow the phrase "architecture of spectatorship" from Anne Friedberg, who in turn notes her debt to the title of a 1999 College Art Association panel organized by Sylvia Lavin, of which Friedberg was a part. Friedberg, *The Virtual Window,* 314 n. 2.

6. Quoted in Youngblood, *Expanded Cinema.*

7. Joselit, *Feedback,* 97.

8. Reiss, *From Margin to Center.* Emphasis added.

9. In retrospect, this argument is spurious since "experience" itself is subject to commodification. For the critique of commodification of experience, see especially Claire Bishop, "Antagonism and Relational Aesthetics," *October* 110 (Fall 2004): 51–79; Rosalind Krauss, "The Cultural Logic of the Late Capitalist Museum," *October* 54 (1990): 3–17; and Miwon Kwon, *One Place after Another: Site-Specific Art and Locational Identity* (Cambridge, Mass.: MIT Press, 2002).

10. While not strictly concerned with the relationship between media screens and constrained participation, numerous art historians and critics have profitably theorized spectator experience (in the form of an obligatory social engagement) as an economic relationship based on the model of the gift. See, for example, Janet Kraynak, "Rikrit Tiravanija's Liability," *Documents* 13 (Fall 1998): 26–40. For an influential analysis not limited to art history, see Alan Schrift, ed., *The Logic of the Gift: Toward an Ethic of Generosity* (New York: Routledge, 1997).

11. Although Nauman has experimented with corridor constructions in a variety of works for more than fifteen years, the vast majority of the self-titled corridor installations were completed between 1969 and 1972.

12. Nauman's screen-reliant corridor pieces include *Video Corridor for San Francisco (Come Piece)* (1969), *Corridor Installation (Installation at Nick Wilder)* (1970), *Four Corner Piece* (1970), *Going around the Corner Piece* (1970), *Going around the Corner Piece with Live and Taped Monitors* (1970), and *Live-Taped Video Corridor* (1970).

13. Lacan's concept of the gaze—first developed as a series of lectures titled "Of the Gaze as *Objet Petit a*" and later published in *The Four Fundamentals of Psychoanalysis*—concerns both the acknowledgment of the presence of others and the process by which subjects seek confirmation of themselves. Jacques Lacan, *The Four Fundamentals of Psychoanalysis*, trans. Alan Sheridan (New York: W. W. Norton, 1978).

14. Parveen Adams, "Bruce Nauman and the Object of Anxiety," *October* 83 (1998): 101.

15. Samuel Weber, "Television: Set and Screen," *Mass Mediauras: Form, Technics, Media* (Stanford, Calif.: Stanford University Press, 1996), 121. Emphasis in original. For Weber, this undecidability is ultimately related to the question of placelessness; he concludes the passage quoted above this way: "but that someone or something remains at an irreducible, indeterminable distance from the television viewer: and this distance splits the 'sameness' of the instant of perception as well as the identity of the place in which such viewing seems to occur" (121).

16. Margaret Morse, *Virtualities: Television, Media Art, and Cyberculture* (Bloomington: Indiana University Press, 1998), 14.

17. Although contemporary audiences are certainly more media savvy and acclimated to video surveillance technologies than were their peers in 1970, the disconnect between the viewer's lived bodily experience and its video representation, as well as the issue of screen-based control of the viewer's movements, remains forceful. The best account of this historical shift in terms of contemporary art practice is *Ctrl [Space]: Rhetorics of Surveillance from Bentham to Big Brother*, ed. Thomas Levin, Ursula Frohne, and Peter Weibel (Cambridge and London: MIT Press, 2002).

18. Regarding the presumption of liveness in relationship to commercial broadcast television, see Samuel Cavell, "The Fact of Television," *Video Culture: A Critical Investigation*, ed. John Hanhardt (Rochester, N.Y.: Visual Studies Workshop Press, 1982); Mary Ann Doane, "Information, Crisis, and Catastrophe," *Logics of Television: Essays in Cultural Criticism*, ed. Patricia Mellencamp (Bloomington: Indiana University Press, 1990); Jane Feuer, "The Concept of Live Television: Ontology as Ideology," *Regarding Television: Critical Approaches—An Anthology*, ed. E. Ann Kaplan, American Film Institute Monograph Series, vol. 2 (Frederick, Maryland: University Publications of America, 1983); Sconce, *Haunted Media;* and Weber, "Television."

19. "Willoughby Sharp Interview with Bruce Nauman (1971)," in *Please Pay Attention Please: Bruce Nauman's Words: Writings and Interviews*, ed. Bruce Nauman and Janet Kraynak (Cambridge, Mass.: MIT Press, 2003), 136–37.

20. As if to guarantee that there could be no facile way for the spectator to achieve a satisfactory screen image/presence, the camera lenses in *Video Corridor for San Francisco* were turned from time to time, rendering it next to impossible for the spectator to keep himself or herself "in view." The fact that Nauman's later screen-reliant corridor installations do away with this additional permutation of camera-monitor relations suggests that Nauman wanted to make the highly constrained relationship between the spectator and the screen more comprehensible (or perhaps that the artist found he could control the terms of the spectator's participation even more effectively when the "rules of engagement" were more clearly delineated).

21. "Willoughby Sharp Interview with Bruce Nauman," *Please Pay Attention Please,* ed. Nauman and Kraynak, 136–37. Nauman's description of the piece is worth quoting in full: "It's really like the corridor pieces only without the corridors. I tried to do something similar, but using television cameras and monitors, and masking part of the lenses on the cameras. . . . If one camera is at one end of the room and the monitor is at the other, then the camera lens can be masked so that an image appears maybe on a third or a quarter of the screen. The camera is sometimes turned on its side, sometimes upside down, and that creates a corridor between the camera and the monitor. You can walk in it and see yourself from the back, but it's hard to stay in the picture because you can't line anything up, especially if the camera is not pointing at the monitor. Then you have to watch the monitor to stay in the picture and at the same time stay in the line of the camera" (136–37).

22. Janet Kraynak, "Dependent Participation: Bruce Nauman's Environments," *Grey Room* 10 (Winter 2003): 29.

23. Alain Touraine, *The Post-Industrial Society: Tomorrow's Social History: Classes, Conflicts, and Culture in Programmed Society,* trans. Leonard F. X. Mayhew (New York: Random House, 1971).

24. According to Crary, video display–based viewing "imposes a highly articulated, coercive apparatus, a prescriptive mode of activity and corporeal regimentation"—what he theorizes to be "the banal legacy of the nineteenth century and the dream fabricated then of the complete bureaucratization of society." Television and the personal computer's terminal screen, in other words, are simply the most recent techniques and locations of capitalist control and productivity via the requirements of sedentarization and passivity. See Jonathan Crary, "Eclipse of the Spectacle," *Art after Modernism: Rethinking Representation,* ed. Brian Wallis (New York; Boston: New Museum of Contemporary Art; D. R. Godine, 1984), 293.

25. Crary, "Eclipse of the Spectacle," 294.

26. For an interesting discussion of Dan Graham's video installations in relationship to the artist's notion of topology, see Eric de Bruyn, "Topological Pathways of Post-Minimalism," *Grey Room* 25 (2006): 32.

27. Dan Graham interview with RoseLee Goldberg, June 1975; quoted in RoseLee Goldberg, "Space as Praxis," *Studio International* 977 (September/October 1975): 134. Emphasis in original.

28. Gilles Deleuze, *Cinema I* and *Cinema II,* trans. Hugh Tomlinson (Minneapolis: University of Minnesota, 1986 and 1989). See also *Bergsonism,* trans. Barbara Habberjam and Hugh Tomlison (New York: Zone Books, 1990).

29. Henri Bergson, *Matter and Memory* (orig. 1896), trans. W. S. Palmer and N. M. Paul (New York: Zone Books, 1988).

30. Colin Gardner explains how Deleuze, following Bergson, understands time as "a stream in which the virtual [the immateriality of memory] is already contained in the actual, the cause in the effect, so that the latter can constantly move on to its new actuality-as-future-anterior." Colin Gardner, "Thinking the Unthinkable: Time, Cinema and the Brain," *Journal of Neuro-Aesthetic Theory* 3 (2008), artbrain.org.

31. Joselit, *Feedback,* 106.

32. Ibid., 163.

33. Jacques Rancière, *The Politics of Aesthetics: The Distribution of the Sensible* (London, New York: Continuum, 2004).

34. Joselit, *Feedback*, 157. See also Anne Wagner, "Performance, Video, and the Rhetoric of Presence," *October* 91 (2000): 59–80. Krauss's theorization of how much early video art is bound up with the psychological condition of narcissism is famously rehearsed in her "Video: The Aesthetics of Narcissism," *October* 1 (1976): 51–64.

3. Installing Time

1. While many works of art clearly require temporal engagements, and the experience of visiting museums itself could be described as "cinematic," the installations considered in this chapter are distinctive for the way in which they self-consciously (and quite literally) put media time and duration on display. Annette Michelson makes an interesting proposition regarding the parallels between the experience of viewing a film and visiting a wax museum in her 1966 essay, "Film and the Radical Aspiration," reprinted in *Film Culture Reader*, 406. On the museological archaeology of cinema and cinematic affective transport, see Giuliana Bruno, *Atlas of Emotion: Journeys in Art, Architecture, and Film* (New York: Verso, 2002), as well as her *Public Intimacy*.

2. Art and media historian Anne-Marie Duguet uses the term "exploratory duration" in passing in describing the time-based aspects of Jeffrey Shaw's oeuvre but leaves the concept undeveloped. Anne-Marie Duguet, *Jeffrey Shaw: A User's Manual: From Expanded Cinema to Virtual Reality* (Karlsruhe: Cantz Verlag and ZKM Museum, 1997), 21. She adopts the term based upon Gérard Genette's notion of performance as having a "procedural duration." Gérard Genette, *L'oeuvre de l'art* (Paris: Éditions du Seuil, 1994), 73.

3. Jameson, *Postmodernism*, 72.

4. Anne Friedberg employs the term "window shopping" as an analogy for the relationship between normative cinematic viewing and the culture of consumption (specifically as rooted in the nineteenth century) in her influential study *Window Shopping: Cinema and the Postmodern* (Berkeley: University of California Press, 1993). Her formulation of contemporary spectatorship will be evaluated in the second half of this chapter.

5. Working in the wake of minimalism's challenges to formal autonomy and the opticality of the image, the instantaneity associated with observing formalist modernist art was thrown into question by many artists in the 1960s and 1970s. Artists embraced the contingencies of time and space and created works that were overtly bound up with the spectator's participatory and temporal experience in the exhibition space, whether or not the individual works of art employed film or video technologies. For the extremely influential art historical argument for minimalism's challenge to spectatorship as correlated to real time and space, see Hal Foster, "The Crux of Minimalism," in *The Return of the Real*.

6. Christine Ross, "The Temporalities of Video: Extendedness Revisited," *Art Journal* 65 (Fall 2006): 83.

7. Le Grice, *Abstract Film and Beyond*, 121. The full excerpt reads: "As with perceptual enquiry, the durational issue in film has become very much concerned with the viewer's changing state as content in itself, rather than with an interior content to

which the viewer reacts." Le Grice and Peter Gidal are the primary theorists of so-called structural-materialist film. See Gidal, *Structural Film Anthology* (London: British Film Institute, 1976).

8. Sharits, "Statement Regarding Multiple Screen/Sound 'Locational' Film Environments — Installations," 79–80.

9. Developed within the context of film studies in the 1970s, apparatus theory is concerned with defining how cinema works as an "institutional apparatus" consisting of a programmed relationship between the film, the film projector, the screen, and the spectator. As described by film theorist Christian Metz in 1975 in his seminal essay "The Imaginary Signifier" (English trans. 1982): "The cinematic institution is not just the cinema industry... it is also the mental machinery—another industry—which spectators 'accustomed to the cinema' have internalized historically and which has adapted them to the consumption of films.... The institution is outside us and inside us, indistinctly collective and intimate, sociological and psychoanalytic." In Metz, *The Imaginary Signifier*, 7. In addition to Metz's essay, key texts on apparatus theory include Baudry, "The Apparatus" and "Ideological Effects of the Basic Cinematographic Apparatus."

10. The term is Obrist's. See Hans-Ulrich Obrist, *Interviews, Vol. 1* (Milan: Charta, 2003), 322.

11. Russell Ferguson, "Trust Me," *Douglas Gordon* (Museum of Contemporary Art) (Cambridge, Mass.: MIT, 2001), 16.

12. David Gordon, "... by way of a statement on the artist's behalf" (a letter to the curators of the exhibition *Wild Walls*, Stedelijk Museum, Amsterdam), in *Douglas Gordon: Kidnapping* (New York: D.A.P./Distributed Art Publishers, 1998), 83.

13. Although it is important to keep in mind the different institutional contexts between Warhol's experimental films and art gallery–based screen-reliant experimental works, the way in which the time one spends with *24 Psycho* is strangely pushed into the future again recalls Warhol's films, such as the approximately eight-hour-long *Empire* (1964). Pamela Lee theorizes the experience of watching Warhol's films in relationship to Hegel's concept of "bad infinity" in her *Chronophobia*. *Empire*, she argues, "performs bad infinity at both internal operations and external reception.... [The film] thus stands as an allegory for time located elsewhere: not only the time of its audience, engaged in business other than that of watching, but the future, anticipated in making one's escape from the theater." Lee, *Chronophobia*, 281, 287.

14. Note that *Mapping the Studio* exists in two versions that should not be confused. In the second version, *Mapping the Studio II with color shift, flip, flop & flip/flop (Fat Chance John Cage)* (2001), the images of Nauman's studio are colored and periodically flip up and down.

15. "Night Moves: The Indifferent Grandeur of Bruce Nauman," *The New Yorker* (January 28, 2002): 94–95.

16. *Mapping the Studio I (Fat Chance John Cage)* was first shown at New York City's DIA:Chelsea in a vast, darkened gallery across the street from the DIA Foundation's main building. The way in which the work was installed at DIA:Chelsea differs slightly from the way it is currently installed at DIA:Beacon (and upon which the above description is based). At DIA:Chelsea, Nauman's video images were projected simultaneously onto four walls and seven rolling office chairs were set in the middle of the

space, allowing audience members to relax, swivel, and/or roll around on them while observing the various projections. Now permanently installed at DIA:Beacon, *Mapping the Studio I* incorporates wall-like screens (as opposed to literal walls) and includes wooden, nonrolling chairs. Also note that the DIA:Beacon installation admits more incidental light than did the DIA:Chelsea version.

17. For an interesting investigation of the artistic consequences of simultaneous transmission to multiple sites specifically in regard to video technology, see Margot Bouman, "Translucent Temporalities: The Ontology of Bruce Nauman's *Mapping the Studio,*" paper delivered at College Art Association Conference, Seattle, Washington, February, 2004. Bouman emphasizes video's ability to simultaneously represent an event occurring in one location across multiple locations or, following Samuel Weber, video's "differential specificity." Samuel Weber, *Mass Mediauras: Form, Technics, Media* (Stanford, Calif.: Stanford University Press, 1996).

18. Collectively, the original unedited footage was forty-two hours. Nauman subsequently edited the seven videos in *Mapping the Studio* to approximately five hours and forty-five minutes each.

19. Extremely patient observers will perceive traces of camera movement in addition to the scattered movement of the various nocturnal studio dwellers. The reasons that these and certain other changes are occasionally perceptible are largely fortuitous. Nauman explains: "Because I wasn't shooting every night, every hour the camera moves a tiny bit. The image changes a little bit every hour regardless of any action that's taking place. I was working in the studio during the day all that time, and I would unconsciously move things around. . . . So the areas that I was shooting tended to get cleaner or to have fewer objects in them over the six hours." Bruce Nauman and Michael Auping, "A Thousand Words: Bruce Nauman Talks about *Mapping the Studio,*" *Artforum* 40, no. 7 (March 2002): 121.

20. Ibid.

21. Ibid.

22. David Hunt, "Doug Aitken: Immoral Video," *Art & Text* 67 (1999–2000): np.

23. "A Thousand Words: Douglas Aitken Talks about electric earth," *Artforum* 38, no. 9 (2000): 161. See also Aitken and Noel Daniel, ed., *Broken Screen: Conversations with Doug Aitken—Expanding the Image Breaking the Narrative* (New York: D.A.P., 2006).

24. Apparently committed to the democratic distribution of her work, Ahtila has released many of her films on DVD, complete with scripts of all dialogue.

25. *Eija-Liisa Ahtila: Fantasized Persons and Taped Conversations* (Helsinki: Crystal Eye: Kiasma Museum of Contemporary Art, 2002). The artist recommends that exhibition venues start the film every full and half hour.

26. Royoux, "Remaking Cinema," in *Cinéma Cinéma,* 26.

27. Jean-Christophe Royoux, "All Around the World," *Art Press* (October 2001): 39.

28. Peter Osborne, "Distracted Reception: Time, Art, and Technology," in *Time Zones: Recent Film and Video,* ed. Jessica Morgan and Gregor Muir (London: Tate, 2004), 72.

29. Birnbaum, *Chronology,* 40.

30. "The subject—what Husserl calls the ego—is what keeps all the levels of such a multidimensional structure together: 'I am always in the present and still in the past,

and already in the future. I'm always here and also elsewhere. I as ego come in between these two modes. I am only in this doubling, and I emerge in this displacement." Birnbaum, *Chronology,* 38. (Quoting Robert Sokolowski, "Displacement and Identity in Husserl's Phenomenology," in *Husserl-Ausgabe und Husserl-Forschung,* ed. S. Ijsseling (London: Kluwer, 1990), 180.)

31. Robert Storr, "Stan Douglas: L'Alienation et la proximité (interview)," *Art Press* 202 (2000): 262.

32. Dominique Païni, "Le cinéma expose: flux contre flux / Movies in the Gallery: Flow on Show," *Art Press* 287 (2003): 29. Païni defers to Bernand Steigler as to the cinematographic nature of consciousness, which is also based on a montage of temporal objects—objects constituted by their movement. Bernand Steigler, *La technique et le temps, le temps du cinéma et la question du mal être* (Paris: Galilée, 2001).

33. Païni, "Le cinéma expose / Movies in the Gallery," 29.

34. Even if on the whole he is more sympathetic than Païni, Birnbaum's praise for media installation art is also measured. Birnbaum makes an especially compelling call for new theoretical methods in his incisive refutation of the critical celebration of outmoded technologies in media art by Rosalind Krauss, among others; see Birnbaum, *Chronology,* especially the final chapter, "Chronometers." See also Krauss, *A Voyage on the North Sea.*

35. In an exhibition catalog essay from 1997 (reprinted in *October* magazine), Païni states his case plainly, describing his critique of "the immobile and collective viewer (chained up in Plato and Diderot), captive in the film theaters of the twentieth-century," such that "the viewer of a contemporary projection installation once again becomes a flâneur, mobile and solitary." ("Should We Put an End to Projection?" 32–33) He subsequently refines this argument in a series of articles in *Art Press,* which will be discussed in the body of this text.

36. Païni, "Le ciné ma expose / Movies in the Gallery," 26.

37. Païni, "Le retour du Flâneur: The Return of the Flâneur," *Art Press* 255 (2000): 39, 41.

38. Bellour, "D'un Autre Cinéma," 5–21.

39. Ibid., 15.

40. Michael Archer, "Video Lives," *Art Monthly* 228 (1999): 2. Archer singles out Shirin Neshat's two-screen installation *Turbulent* (1998) as a work that takes this mode of viewing into account, so that the viewer's discomfort in observing the piece is presumably integral to the meaning of the work itself.

41. Even if, in actual practice, viewers appear to be emboldened by the institution and by the presumed etiquette of the "white cube" to enter and leave film and video installations, including pieces like *Consolation Service,* at any time, the critical gesture bound up with the work's *ideal* spectatorship is noteworthy. For a discussion of contemporary media artworks that deliberately encourage the cinematic possibilities of imaginary identification and fantasy, see, for example, Amelia Jones, *Self/Image,* especially chapter 6, "The Televisual Architecture of the Dream Body," and Maria Walsh, "Cinema in the Gallery—Discontinuity and Potential Space in Salla Tykkä's Trilogy," *Senses of Cinema* 28 (September/October 2003): np.

42. Hall and Fifer, "Complexities of an Art Form," in *Illuminating Video: An Essential Guide to Video Art,* 20.

43. *Illuminating Video,* ed. Hall and Fifer, 20.

44. Chrissie Iles, "Roundtable: The Projected Image," *October* 104 (2003): 94, my emphasis.

45. Prominent exceptions include David Joselit, "Inside the Light Cube," *Artforum* (2004): 154–59; Liz Kotz, "Video: The Space between Screens," in *Theory in Contemporary Art since 1985,* ed. Simon Leung and Zoya Kocur (London: Basil Blackwell, 2004); and Kraynak, "Dependent Participation."

46. Krauss, "The Cultural Logic of the Late Capitalist Museum," 3–17.

47. Put simply, minimalism's quest for the "death of the author" was not supposed to mean a corresponding total empowerment of the spectator. Nonetheless, minimalism's "immediacy," explains Krauss, was always "potentially undermined—infected, we could say—with its opposite." Krauss, "The Cultural Logic of the Late Capitalist Museum," 287. See also Foster, "The Crux of Minimalism."

48. Païni, "Le retour du Flâneur: The Return of the Flâneur," 39 and 41.

49. Ibid., 41.

50. For example, in the *Artforum* article devoted to Nauman's description of *Mapping the Studio I (Fat Chance John Cage),* Nauman makes pointed remarks about the intended spectatorship for this work that closely correspond to the way in which viewers tend to observe the omnipresent media screens in contemporary life. Nauman has this advice for his spectator–participants: "If you try and concentrate on or pay attention to a particular spot in the image, you'll miss something. So you really have to not concentrate and allow your peripheral vision to work. You tend to get more if you just scan without seeking. You have to become passive, I think." Nauman would appear to be asking his spectators to enjoy this work in a manner most closely approximating the experience of "flow" that Marxist critic Raymond Williams famously associated with television. Nauman and Auping, "A Thousand Words," 121.

51. Friedberg, *Window Shopping,* 143. Friedberg revisits this argument in her "The End of Cinema: Multimedia and Technological Change," in *Film Theory and Criticism,* ed. Leo Baudry (New York: Oxford University Press, 2004). See also Paul Virilio's discussion of the VCR in "The Third Window" (interview) in *Global Television,* ed. Cynthia Schneider and Brian Wallis (Cambridge, Mass.: MIT Press, 1988), as well as Laura Mulvey, *Death 24x a Second: Stillness and the Moving Image* (London: Reaktion Books, 2006) on the contemporary viewer's gratifyingly easy access to repetition, slow motion, and the freeze-frame.

52. *Loop* (exh. cat.), ed. Klaus Biesenbach (Munich: Kunsthalle der Hypo-Kulturstiftung, 2001).

4. Be Here (and There) Now

1. Some exceptions are works by Anthony McCall, Paul Sharits, Fabio Mauri, Joan Jonas, Michael Snow, and Robert Whitman.

2. The notion that the viewing subject constructed by Renaissance perspective remained unchanged throughout modernity has been challenged on many fronts. Crary's *Techniques of the Observer* and Hubert Damisch's *The Origin of Perspective* (Cambridge, Mass.: MIT Press, 1994) are particularly useful for considering these shifts in relationship to technologies of visualization.

3. See, for example, Benjamin Buchloh, "Sculpture and Process in Richard Serra's Films," in *Richard Serra: Works '66–'77* (Tubingen: Kunsthalle, 1978); Regina Cornwell, "Paul Sharits: Illusion and Object," *Artforum* 10 (1971): 56–62, and "Michael Snow," in *Projected Images;* Krauss, "Paul Sharits," 89–102, and "Richard Serra: Sculpture," in *Richard Serra: Sculpture* (exh. cat.) (New York: Museum of Modern Art, 1986); Annette Michelson, "Paul Sharits and the Critique of Illusionism: An Introduction," *Film Culture* (1978): 83–88, and "Toward Snow," *Artforum* 9 (June 1971): 30–37. The catalog for the 1974 *Projected Images* exhibition offers a useful entry point to evaluate the early North American critical reception of film and video installation; evaluating works by Peter Campus, Rockne Krebs, Paul Sharits, Michael Snow, Ted Victoria, and Robert Whitman, the writers are united by their emphasis on what they identify as a sculptural or environmental quality to the works, a concern with process, and the spectator's alleged transformation into an active "participant." (Interestingly, the now widely accepted term "projected images" was not favored by any of the writers, despite its use in the show's title.) For a recent historical account of postminimalism and film, see Eric Le Bruyn, "The Expanded Field of Cinema, or Exercise on the Perimeter of a Square," in *X-Screen: Film Installation and Actions in the 1960s and 1970s* (exh. cat.), ed. Matthias Michalka (Koln: Verlag der Buchhandlung Walther Konig, 2003).

4. Filmmaker and theorist Peter Gidal proposed the term "structural-materialist" film in 1975 to distinguish conceptual and materialist works that seek to expose their own ideological operations from the variant of "North American" structural film, famously identified in P. Adams Sitney's 1969 landmark essay on the genre, whose exclusive concern, according to Gidal, was the largely formalist modernist project of investigating the "filmic" qualities of film. Key practitioners associated with structural-materialist film included Hollis Frampton, Kurt Kren, Peter Kubelka, Malcolm LeGrice, William Raban, Sharits, and Snow. See Gidal, "Theory and Definition of Structural/Materialist Film," 189–96, and *Structural Film Anthology*, and Le Grice, *Abstract Film and Beyond* and *Film as Film: Formal Experiment in Film* (exh. cat.), ed. Birgit Hein and Wulf Herzogenrath (London: Arts Council of Great Britain, 1979). Peter Wollen's highly influential critique of structural-materialist film describes what he takes to be the art form's theoretical and political deficiencies, even as the terms of his critique tended to collapse the significant differences among variants of so-called structural film. See Wollen, "The Two Avant-Gardes," *Studio International* 190, no. 978 (1975): 171–75; and "'Ontology' and 'Materialism' in Film," *Screen* 17 (1976): 7–23.

5. See Baudry, "Ideological Effects of the Basic Cinematographic Apparatus." Baudry refines this line of critique in his more psychoanalytically informed 1975 essay "The Apparatus."

6. Since the 1970s, critics, historians, and especially feminist film theorists have criticized apparatus theory for what were taken to be sweeping, ahistorical generalizations—including a generalized, ungendered account of subjectivity—and for theorizing spectatorship in such a way as to leave no room for oppositional practices or resistance.

7. Although strictly concerned with mainstream cinema, Roland Barthes theorizes a related type of spectatorial doubleness (what he calls an "amorous distance") in his "Leaving the Movie Theater," 345–49.

8. Fried, "Art and Objecthood," 12–23.

9. Wollen's well-known theorization of two separate filmic avant-gardes—a for-malist avant-garde associated with the Co-op movement and especially associated with the "essentialism" of structural film, and an overtly "political" avant-garde associated with filmmakers such as Jean-Luc Godard—is at the core of many of these debates. Wollen, "The Two Avant-Gardes," 171–75.

10. Anne Friedberg, "The Virtual Window," *Rethinking Media Change: The Aesthetics of Transition,* ed. David Thorburn and Henry Jenkins (Cambridge, Mass.: MIT Press, 2003), 337–54, and *The Virtual Window.* Although Friedberg devotes a chapter of her book to "exceptions" to the dominant virtual window model (including certain visual artworks), she contends that the spatially and temporally fractured frames proposed by the multiple and overlapping screens that characterize the Windows operating system inaugurate a fundamentally *new* form of visuality.

11. Manovich, *The Language of New Media.*

12. I borrow the term "warped space" from Anthony Vidler. Vidler theorizes the history of "warped" psychological and artistic spaces extending from the nineteenth century to the present in *Warped Space: Art, Architecture, and Anxiety in Contemporary Culture* (Cambridge, Mass.: MIT Press, 2000).

13. The pioneering text here is Metz, *The Imaginary Signifier.* See also my discussion of film theory as it pertains to media art spectatorship in chapter 1 [note 33].

14. Media scholar and artist Erkki Huhtamo has written a detailed history of the cultural function of screens that carefully attends to transitions in material forms. See Huhtamo, "Elements of Screenology," 31–82.

15. It is interesting to note that Ping-Pong emerged as a privileged cultural trope in the 1960s–1970s. U.S. players invited to Beijing for an international table tennis competition in 1971 constituted the first group of Americans allowed into China since the Communist takeover in 1949, which proved a catalyst to thawing relations between the two countries and ultimately led to Nixon's visit to China in 1971. (*Time* magazine described the sporting event as "the ping heard round the world" and the metaphor "ping pong diplomacy" followed shortly after). I thank Judith Rodenbeck for this reference. Atari introduced the screen-based virtual equivalent of Ping-Pong with its seminal video game PONG (originally an arcade coin-op) in 1972, variants of which had been in development since the late 1950s.

16. Miriam Hansen has examined Walter Benjamin's extremely provocative but lesser-known work on the playfully disruptive capacities of film technology. "Spiel, *[play],*" explains Hansen, "provides Benjamin with a term, and concept, that allows him to imagine an alternative mode of aesthetics on a par with modern, collective experience, an aesthetics that could counteract, at the level of sense perception, the political consequences of the failed . . . reception of technology." Most relevant to the current argument, Benjamin extended the concept of play *[spiel]* to, in Hansen's words, "the behaviour of the spectating collective in front of the screen, including involuntary, sensory-motor forms of reception." Miriam Hansen, "Room-for-Play: Benjamin's Gamble with Cinema," *October* 109 (2004): 3–45.

17. The artist's creation of an alternate version of *Ping Pong* using a television screen later the same year suggests that EXPORT's principal interest was in challenging the viewer's experience with media screens in general as opposed to cinema in particu-

lar. In the spirit of Duchamp and Fluxus, EXPORT even advertised a do-it-yourself, ready-made version of the installation in *Film* magazine in 1969. Titled *Ping Pong Kassette*, the work included a ball, paddle, and 8 mm film (as shown in the relevant figure) whereas the consumer presumably supplied his or her own projector and screen.

18. EXPORT in *Wien: Bildkompendium Wiener Aktionismus und Film*, ed. Peter Weibel (Frankfurt/Main: Kohlkunstverlag, 1970), 262.

19. The desired creation of a progressive, "democratic," and presumably critical spectatorship via obligatory participation is a paradox of much installation art. For two interesting accounts of how art historians are beginning to rethink the critical discourse around spectator participation in relationship to installation art, see Kraynak's "Dependent Participation," 22–45, and Judith Rodenbeck's "Madness and Method: Before Theatricality" (*Grey Room* 13 (2003): 54–79). Branden Joseph theorizes a divergent historical model of theatricality stemming from the legacy of John Cage in *Beyond the Dream Syndicate*, especially chapter 2, "The Social Turn."

20. See especially "The Modern Theatre Is the Epic Theatre" and "A Short Organum for the Theater" in *Brecht on Theatre*, trans. John Willett (New York: Hill and Wang, 1978), 33–42 and 179–205. See also Walter Benjamin, "The Author as Producer," in *The Essential Frankfurt School Reader*, ed. Andrew Arato and Eike Gebhardt (New York: Urizen Books, 1978), 254–69. His alienation effect and theorization of the apparatus were deeply influential for film and media artists and critics in the late 1960s and early 1970s. Peter Wollen explicitly critiques the (mis)reception of Brechtian aesthetics within the context of structural-materialist film in his influential 1976 essay, "'Ontology' and 'Materialism' in Film." Wollen argues that these media practitioners, in what amounted to a misappropriation of post-Brechtian aesthetics, misapprehended the critical value of "materialism" by collapsing an emphasis on materiality and filmic materials (anti-illusionism broadly conceived) with the critical gesture of political materialism (in the specific post-Brechtian sense).

21. David Joselit, "The Video Public Sphere," *Art Journal* 59, no. 2 (Summer 2000): 48. See also his *Feedback*, especially chapters 3 and 4.

22. See Adams, "Bruce Nauman and the Object of Anxiety," 96–113, for a detailed exploration of the phenomenological and psychoanalytical valences of Bruce Nauman's artistic production, including his influential video installations.

23. Lacan, "The Mirror Stage as Formative of the Function of the I as Revealed in Psychoanalytic Experience." Lacan's theory of vision is most fully developed, however, in his series of lectures titled "Of the Gaze as *Objet Petit a*" and collected in *The Four Fundamentals of Psychoanalysis*. On the considerable misinterpretation of Lacan's model of vision and specifically within film theory, see Joan Copjec, *Read My Desire: Lacan against the Historicists* (Cambridge and London, UK: MIT Press, 1995).

24. Looking back on this period in a 1996 essay, Le Grice discerns an emphasis on screen-based experimentation and confirms that "the language or discourse of cinema is fundamentally altered—philosophically and in the social/cultural arena—by emerging forms which first establish the screen as surface then reverse the symbolic space from behind to before the screen." Although Le Grice recognizes the pivotal role of the screen in these works, his formulation is incomplete. Screen-reliant installations such as those by EXPORT and Campus grapple with (at least) three screen spaces simultaneously:

the space behind the screen, the space before the screen, and, finally, the spatial presence of the screen object itself. Le Grice, "Mapping in Multispace: Expanded Cinema to Virtuality," in *White Cube/Black Box: Video, Installation, Film* (exh. cat.), ed. Sabine Breitweiser (Vienna: Generali Foundation, 1996), 267.

5. What Lies Ahead

1. Beyond its more recent association with digital media technologies, the term "virtual" has a rich and complex history in critical philosophy since the late nineteenth century in texts by Jean Baudrillard, Henri Bergson, Gilles Deleuze, Felix Guattari, Pierre Lévy, Paul Virilio, and others (although one could locate the roots of this discourse as early as Plato's writings on the simulacrum). In this chapter, I follow Anne Friedberg's working definition of the term "virtual," which she defines as that which "serves to distinguish between any representation or appearance (whether optically, technologically, or artisanally produced) that appears 'functionally or effectively *but not formally*' of the same materiality as that which it represents. Virtual images have a materiality and a reality but of a different kind, a second-order materiality, liminally immaterial. The terms 'original' and 'copy' will not apply here, because the virtuality of the image does not imply direct mimesis, but a transfer—more like metaphor—from one plane of meaning and appearance to another." Friedberg, *The Virtual Window*, 11.

2. While this chapter focuses exclusively on artworks conceived of and executed with digital computer screens, it is important to note that artists have experimented with incorporating computer technologies into artworks since the mid-1960s, including practices as diverse as expanded cinema, media events and actions, cybernetic artworks, and, more recently, net art. Also worth mentioning is how, in recent years, artworks originally executed in film and video are routinely reconfigured in digital formats for the purposes of publicity and/or exhibition; intentionally or otherwise, this decision echoes the omnipresence of computer technologies in daily life. For a cogent treatment of digital media in the institutional context of the visual arts, see *Net_Condition: Art and Global Media* (exh. cat.), ed. Timothy Druckrey and Peter Weibel (Cambridge and London: MIT Press and ZKM | Center for Art and Media, 2001).

3. On telepresence in media art see especially Lev Manovich, "To Lie and to Act: Potemkin's Villages, Cinema, and Telepresence," in *The Robot in the Garden: Telerobotics and Telepistemology in the Age of the Internet*, ed. Ken Goldberg (Cambridge, Mass.: MIT Press, 2000), 164–79. See also his *Language of New Media*, 99–102, which documents the ways in which screens have been employed to directly affect reality in various military applications from radar to interactive computer graphics.

4. Media scholar Ron Burnett proposes that virtual images occupy a "middle space" by combining the virtual and the real into conceptually ambiguous visual environments in *How Images Think* (Cambridge, Mass.: MIT Press, 2005).

5. Computer gaming—in which players are active participants in remote *virtual* screen-based realms—presents an interesting border case here. On the cultural ramifications of gaming see Alex Galloway, *Gaming: Essays on Algorithmic Culture* (Minneapolis: University of Minnesota Press, 2006) and McKenzie Wark, *Gamer Theory* (Cambridge, Mass.: Harvard University Press, 2007). While it falls outside the scope of the current study, the burgeoning realm of mobile computing and gaming that requires users to

engage with screens in a haptic fashion while engrossed in multiple spaces offers a rich subject for future research. For a preliminary analysis along these lines, see Andreas Gregersen and Torben Grodal, "Embodiment and Interface," in Bernard Perro and Robert Wolfe, ed., *The Video Game Theory Reader 2* (London: Routledge, 2009).

6. Oliver Grau, *Virtual Art: From Illusion to Immersion* (Cambridge, Mass.: MIT Press, 2003), 285.

7. Friedberg, *The Virtual Window,* 235.

8. Hershman and the Internet design company Construct were announced co-winners when *The Difference Engine #3* won the Ars Electronica Golden Nica Award in 1999.

9. Paul Virilio traces the disturbing connections between the subject's relationship to war and to media forms in *War and Cinema: The Logistics of Perception* (London: Verso, 1989).

10. On the question of "immersion" and "interactivity" in relationship to gallery-based media art, see Grau, *Virtual Art; Morse, Virtualities; Immersed in Technology: Art and Virtual Environments,* ed. Mary Ann Moser and Douglas MacLeod (Cambridge, Mass.: MIT Press, 1996); *Multimedia: From Wagner to Virtual Reality,* ed. Randall Packer and Ken Jordan (New York: W. W. Norton, 2001); and *Critical Issues in Electronic Media,* ed. Simon Penny (New York: SUNY Press, 1995).

11. The intertitle "Two-Way Mirror Power" is a deliberate reference to the title of an influential book about Dan Graham that makes extended reference to the artist's participatory and experiential installations, many of which were influential precedents for the artworks assessed in this chapter and throughout this book. Dan Graham, *Two-Way Mirror Power: Selected Writings by Dan Graham on His Art,* ed. Alexander Alberro (Cambridge, Mass.: MIT Press and Marian Goodman Gallery, 1999).

12. When the BBU screens are inactive for an extended period, a "Siren"-type screensaver image appears on the BBU screens that beckons observers to engage with the work. If viewers succumb to the Siren's advances and physically manipulate the screen objects, the screensaver disappears and the screen returns to featuring selected "virtual" images of the physical museum.

13. Each museum visitor's captured image travels on a three-stage journey through the virtual environment conceptualized as "inside" *The Difference Engine #3*'s screens. First, each spectator image-cum-avatar briefly passes through the graphically rendered museum corridors shown on the BBUs. This part of the avatar's journey can be seen by any online or museum viewer who happens to be looking at any of the computer screens during the avatar's thirty-second cycle through Hershman's diagrammatic representation of the museum space. Next, the avatar pauses for one hour in what Hershman calls "Purgatory," the intermediate stage of the journey where the visitors' faces are automatically and temporarily transferred from the BBU screens onto the display screen positioned immediately inside the museum. What Hershman calls the "Archive" proper is the third and final stage of the captured image's virtual journey. Upon leaving Purgatory, the spectator images are permanently archived, irrevocably rendered components of this digital realm and stored in a virtual environment on the artwork's Web site.

14. Goldberg's description of the project nevertheless acknowledges the fragility of the work's objective of long-term cooperative virtual gardening: "Strangers will rub shoulders with strangers, raising questions of cooperation versus competition in the

use of limited resources. The garden could evolve as a green and blooming oasis, or it could become a barren plot. The garden's future has been left up to its 'gardeners.'" Goldberg cited in E. Mankin, 1995; news release, University of Southern California, June 1995.

15. This raises a related question about the "lifespan" of Internet-based works. While neither project is currently functional, aspects of both continue to exist in documentary form on the Internet.

16. Researchers at the University of Southern California's Annenberg School of Communications conducted a series of empirical studies on "community building" in relationship to *The Telegarden*. See Margaret McLaughlin, Kerry Osborne, and Nicole Ellison, "Virtual Community in a Telepresence Environment," in *Virtual Culture: Identity and Communication in Cybersociety*, ed. Steven Jones (London: Sage Publications, 1997). It is worth noting that the larger critical discourse on the question of "community building" in relationship to contemporary art has problematized many of these assumptions. See, for example, Rosalyn Deutsche, *Evictions: Art and Spatial Politics* (Cambridge, Mass.: MIT Press, 1996); Kwon, *One Place after Another: Site-Specific Art and Locational Identity;* and Bishop, "Antagonism and Relational Aesthetics," 51–79.

17. Mitchell, "Replacing Place," in *The Digital Dialectic: New Essays on New Media,* ed. Peter Lunenfeld (Cambridge, Mass.: MIT Press, 1999), 127.

18. Ibid., 126.

19. Manovich, *The Language of New Media,* 90.

20. Vidler, *Warped Space,* 236.

21. Elizabeth Grosz, *Architecture from the Outside: Essays on Virtual and Real Space* (Cambridge, Mass.: MIT Press, 2001), 88.

22. Deleuze, *Difference and Repetition* (New York: Columbia University Press, 1994). According to Deleuze, "For Ideas, to be actualised is to be differenciated. In themselves and in their virtuality they are thus completely undifferentiated. (In this sense the virtual is by no means a vague notion, but one which possesses full objective reality; it cannot be confused with the possible which lacks reality. As a result, whereas the possible is the mode of identity of concepts within representation, the virtual is the modality of the differential at the heart of Ideas)" (279). Deleuze later uses the term "virtual" to help distinguish the two sides of what he deems the cinema's "crystal-image" (the "actual" and the "virtual") in *Cinema 2: The Time Image,* trans. Hugh Tomlinson and Robert Galeta (Minneapolis: University of Minnesota Press, 1989).

23. Deleuze's concept borrows from Henri Bergson's *Matter and Memory,* in which the philosopher famously theorized matter as an aggregate of images: "And by image we mean a certain existence which is more than that which the idealist calls a representation, but less than that which the realist calls a thing—an existence placed halfway between the 'thing' and its 'representation.'" Bergson, *Matter and Memory,* 9–10.

24. Herbert Dreyfus, "Telepistemology: Descartes's Last Stand," in *The Robot in the Garden,* ed. Goldberg, 54.

25. Ibid.

26. Michael Heim, *The Metaphysics of Virtual Reality* (New York: Oxford University Press, 1994), 97.

27. Albert Borgmann, "Information, Nearness, and Farness," in *The Robot in the Garden,* ed. Goldberg, 90–107. See also Borgmann, *Holding on to Reality: The Nature*

of Information at the Turn of the Millennium (Chicago: University of Chicago Press, 1999).

28. To the extent that artworks simply "bracket out" the body and personal presence by (to use Heim's words) "omitting or simulating corporeal immediacy," they may inadvertently contribute to the disembodying of contemporary viewing subjects and the seeming "dematerialization" of the viewer-screen interface. See Heim, *The Metaphysics of Virtual Reality*, 100. Heim's cautionary remarks are apt: "The stand-in self can never fully represent us. The more we mistake the cyberbodies for ourselves, the more the machine twists ourselves into the prostheses we are wearing" (101).

Afterword

1. Friedberg, *The Virtual Window*, 7.

2. Morse, *Virtualities*, 119.

3. Walter Benjamin, "The Work of Art in the Age of Mechanical Reproduction," in *Illuminations*, ed. Hannah Arendt (New York: Schocken Books, 1968), 217–51.

4. Hansen, "Room-for-Play," 45.

5. For example, although it is beyond the scope of the present inquiry, there is a need for a book-length study of the deployment of "artistic" screens situated in urban, ambient spaces outside of the art gallery's "white cube." Giuliana Bruno, Anne Friedberg, Anna McCarthy, and Margaret Morse, among others, have begun this important work (as detailed in the book's introduction), although there is more to be done on identifying the spectatorship associated with experiencing large-scale public art projections, interactive video installations, and the multitude of artistic and/or commercial moving images sited on architectural surfaces of all kinds. The International Urban Screens Association investigates the commercial use of outdoor screens in combination with "cultural content." See http://www.urbanscreens.org/.

6. The Variable Media Network (initially known as the Variable Media Initiative, sponsored by the Guggenheim Museum and spearheaded by curator John Hanhardt) and the biannual "Orphan Film Symposium," directed by film scholar Dan Streible and affiliated with New York University, are among the better-known institutional efforts dedicated to addressing issues of preservation and obsolescence among screen-based media arts. http://variablemedia.net/

7. Crary, "Eclipse of the Spectacle," 290.

8. Ibid., 294.

Index

Acconci, Vito, 37, 39

Adams, Parveen, 29, 34

Ahtila, Eija-Liisa, xii, 40; *Consolation Service,* xix, 49–51, 52, 53, 112n24; experimental films of, 51

Aitken, Doug, xii, 40; *electric earth,* xix, 41, 47–49, 53

Alberti, Leon Battista, xiii, 63

alienation: Marxist critique of, 25; of subject, 34

Archer, Michael, 55, 113n40

art: community building in, 120n16; fin-de-siècle, 55; premodern, 98n7; public, 121n5; relationship to cinema, xvi; screen-based, xi–xiii, xv, 1; spectatorship for, xii, 25, 64; temporal engagements with, 110n1. *See also* closed-circuit video installations; installation art, screen-reliant

art history: digital art in, 79; gaze in, 98n10; installation art in, xv; museum audiences in, 56; on post-medium condition, 100n20; screens in, xvii, 101n23; spectatorship in, 93, 95, 98n10, 107n10

art institutions: media screens in, xi–xiii, xvi, xviii, 6, 62, 63; reflexivity about, 98n8; temporality of, 56. *See also* galleries

attention: coerced, 35; cultural foundations of, 22; psychological explanations of, 22–23; regulation of, 23; of spectators, 21–24; technologies of, 35, 39

avatars, digital, 81, 119n13

Barthes, Roland, 115n6; "Leaving the Movie Theater," 19

Bateson, Gregory, 103n12

Baudrillard, Jean, 77, 79

Baudry, Jean-Louis, 61, 74

Bellour, Raymond, 55

Benjamin, Walter, 116n16; "The Work of Art in the Age of Mechanical Reproduction," 94–95

Bergson, Henri: on images, 120n23; on time, 36, 109n30

bidirectional browsing units (BBUs), 81, 82

Biesenbach, Klaus: *Loop,* 58

Birnbaum, Daniel, 40; *Chronology,* 53, 100n19; on the subject, 112n30

black boxes: in galleries, xii

body–screen interfaces, xviii, xix, xxi, 17, 41; coercive, 21, 24, 35; materiality of, 69; spatial aspects of, 69, 75; temporal aspects of, 39. *See also* viewer–screen interfaces

Kate Mondloch is assistant professor of art history at the University of Oregon.